# DISTRACTED BY SUCCESS

## ARE YOU ON THE ROAD TO A LIFE WITH NO REGRETS?

# BRANDON BUCK

INFINITE
STRENGTHS

Published by:
Infinite Strengths Publishing
PO Box 19
Livermore CO 80536

Copyright © 2024
ISBN: 978-1-961194-22-9
Printed in the United States of America

# FOREWORD

A Lifelong Learner

"Moses spent 40 years thinking he was somebody, 40 years learning he was nobody, and 40 years discovering what God could do with a nobody."

Brandon and I were introduced to one another by Jay Bell in 2014. Jay was moonlighting as a High School baseball coach and groundskeeper as well as being the Pittsburgh Pirates Hitting Coach in 2013.

Jay had mentioned I needed to meet Brandon Buck. Jay shared with me that Brandon had a gift for leading men. Young and old. He could provide me with an opportunity to spend some time with Brandon if I were to speak at his High School Baseball Team's Banquet.

We have stayed in contact since. I just wanted you to know we've been friends for ten years and have leaned into each other for advice (we have plenty) and wisdom (not so much).

We've gotten to know each other's families and pray for each other as husbands, dads, leaders, friends, and lifelong learners. We've shared lessons learned, failures, strategies, laughs, and challenges.

In 2022, Brandon asked me to speak at a Leadership Summit he was hosting in Boise, Idaho. The Summit, otherwise known as "The Standard," had a small but impactful list of speakers. I was humbled to be a part of an event that just had a good feel to it.

So it's now 2024, and Brandon is writing a book, "Distracted by Success". He reached out and asked if I would write the foreword. I've not written a book; however, I've been blessed to have written a few forewords and many endorsements. I asked Brandon to send me the rough draft, and I'd read it and then let him know if I was in on helping.

Getting this to Brandon took me longer than it should've. I became "Distracted by the Success" I felt this book was going to have, and I would not start writing this forward until I read the book completely.

And then Brandon sent me the trailer. C'mon man! This book is a masterclass (hot term) in leadership, learning, and teaching.

So many quality shares. The list of leaders he sculled from is eye-opening.

I love John Wooden, and he is included.

Here is a share and some notes from Wooden's Wisdom Newsletter that capture the traits I admire about Brandon.... and why you should buy this book.

## IT TAKES TRUST, FAITH, AND PATIENCE TO ACQUIRE PEACE OF MIND AND NOT BE DISTRACTED BY SUCCESS

When people are considering a relationship or doing business with you, one of the first things they want to know is whether or not they can trust you.

Trust can mean different things to different people.

Here are Coach Wooden's thoughts, as noted by Jay Carty:

Sincerity: We cannot become successful unless we interact with others. Sincerity is the mortar that binds together the blocks of friendship, loyalty, cooperation, and team spirit.

Honesty: Honesty is doing the things that we know are right and not giving in to the temptation to do the things that we know are wrong. Honesty must occur at all times, in both thought and action. Honest people stay on the narrow way, regardless of the consequences.

Reliability: When we are reliable, others know that they can depend on us. They know that we will make the effort to do our best, whatever the situation might be. Reliability earns the respect of those around us.

Integrity: Integrity, in its simplest form, is purity of intention. It's keeping a clean conscience.

Purity of intention is really a reflection of the heart. The heart of a person with integrity always wants to do what's right once he or she is sure what "right" is. When we have integrity, we are not going to do anything that will be demeaning to anybody else.

People with integrity are, as Coach said, genuinely concerned about the betterment of others.

To evaluate a relationship, ask yourself if the other person would describe you as sincere, honest, reliable, and full of integrity.

This sums up my feelings about Brandon Buck.
I trust him.
He's sincere.
He's honest.
He's reliable.
He has integrity.

I've even read the bibliography.
When you read "Distracted by Success," you will be better.
Brandon hasn't stopped coaching. He helps you help yourself to be the "best you" you've ever been.

# HOW TO READ THIS BOOK.

Thank you so much for purchasing Distracted by Success. I am humbled and honored that you took a chance on me. My desire is that this book provides as much value as possible. So, I want to explain how it is laid out and what you can expect when reading through it.

Distracted by Success is divided into stages. I broke down each stage into three chapters. The first chapter of each stage discusses distractions that deceive so many of us. The second chapter discusses how successful people address these distractions and cut them out of their lives. Finally, the third chapter, in each stage, introduces a plan you can adapt, follow, and implement to best help you start living a life with no more regrets.

This book could be a quick read, but I encourage you to take your time. It would be best if you read with a pen in hand. Answer the questions as you go. Put aside time for reflection. Set action plans along the way and put yourself to work in your daily life. Make a commitment to yourself to complete the entire book and really reflect on how you are living and can live better going forward. There will be calls to action; take them! The magic of this book will come from your reflection, plan setting, implementation, and efforts, not from the book's content. So, decide right now to commit, or don't waste your time continuing to read.

We created a Distracted by Success webpage that includes all the questions within the book (if you would rather print them out), links to assessments mentioned in the book, other helpful resources, and a link to the Distracted by Success Facebook page. This FB page is only for leaders who have read this book and are committed to living a life of true success and want to gain and give encouragement along the way.

Distracted by Success Website –

https://infinitestrengths.com/distracted-by-success/

Facebook Page –

www.facebook.com/groups/distractedbysuccess/

# HERE IS HOW THE BOOK IS ORGANIZED.

# DISTRACTED
# BY
# SUCCESS

ARE YOU ON THE ROAD
TO A LIFE WITH NO REGRETS?

# INTRODUCTION:
## THE ROAD TO SUCCESS

# INTRODUCTION: ROAD TO SUCCESS
## CHAPTER 1: DISTRACTED SUCCESS

*"I think everybody should get rich and famous and do everything they ever dreamed of so they can see that it's not the answer."*
Jim Carrey

## WHAT IS YOUR DEFINITION OF SUCCESS? (WRITE IT HERE)

## WHAT DOES IT MEAN TO BE SUCCESSFUL?

Does someone achieve success once they earn a big corner office, win a championship ring, or grow a massive bank account? Is success achieved once you get married, have children, own the biggest house in the neighborhood or drive the fanciest car? Is success about acquiring as much stuff as possible, regardless of need? Does success require that you do whatever is necessary to achieve your goals, regardless of ethics? Is success only reserved for a few? Is success so elusive that it is rarely achieved? Is becoming successful like throwing mud at a wall and hoping it sticks?

Success is the thing that every one of us wants, but very few can clearly define what it means to achieve it.

## WHAT SUCCESS IS NOT

Success isn't some unobtainable goal; it isn't derived from your financial statements, nor is it based on how attractive your spouse is or what type of car you drive. Success isn't dependent upon your championships, titles, or accolades. And success certainly is not about popularity, how talented your children are, or how many degrees you have.

## WHAT SUCCESS IS

Success is, however, about how you live your life. It is about discovering who you are, loving people, constantly seeking to get better, and then bringing your true identity everywhere you go. Success is about how you think and respond to the unexpected curveballs that life will inevitably throw at you. Success is most certainly about how you treat and interact with people. Success is about building something that helps you and those around you to be their best, even if that means they become better than you.

Unfortunately, too many of us have become so distracted by the temptation of power, money, fame, influence, and opinions that we end up living a life of regret. We chase these false idols in hopes that they will provide us with purpose and meaning, but only to find that these material things leave us feeling empty and wanting more. We gain accolades and notoriety only to get to the end of our lives, realizing that these distractions caused us to miss the point of everything.

Just look at the world of college football. Here, coaches have dedicated their entire lives to the sport. Many sacrifice their families, health, friendships, and their youth to spend endless hours creating plans, recruiting players, working on development, hiring coaches, designing offensive and defensive schemes, addressing issues, enforcing discipline, and a multitude of other things. For many or most, this is all done in the name of winning. The siren song of a championship, a banner, or a ring keeps calling, and they believe that winning will justify everything. That it will provide them with a meaningful purpose and guarantee their longevity.

But here is the thing: it doesn't! That is the distraction. Sure, winning games, championships, or titles are great, and I certainly want to win, expect to win, and will bust my tail to win. Let me be clear: this desire or expectation to win is not the distraction. Winning is a distraction when it becomes the main or the only thing. It (and so many other things in this life) is a distraction when we sacrifice all the other aspects of our lives to achieve it.

Think about it. When you win, how long does the euphoria last? How long does winning feel like enough? A month, a week, a day, a couple of hours? When the feeling is gone, then what? Most often, we feel empty. We long for that dopamine to hit again, and some fear it will never come. So, we sacrifice even more to get it.

**HOW LONG DOES WINNING FEEL LIKE ENOUGH?**

Though impressive and needed, winning, selling, performing, or achieving are not outcomes entirely within our control. The lack of control, coupled with the internal and external expectations to win, increases pressure, which will often cause many of us to do whatever it takes to win, regardless of ethics or morality. Let's say you do win but cheated or did something illegal. Did you really win? Is it worth it when you might spend the rest of your life worrying that someone will find out what you did? If you win, yet do not have a strong family, have no close friends, or miss your children growing up, did you really win? Are you truly successful if you gain the world yet lose your soul in the process?

**IF YOU WIN, YET DO NOT HAVE A STRONG FAMILY, HAVE NO CLOSE FRIENDS, OR MISS YOUR CHILDREN GROWING UP, DID YOU REALLY WIN?**

What if you do win, and you do it with integrity? Does that guarantee anything? Does winning ensure longevity or job security? No, it does not. Recall former legendary Chicago Bulls coach Phil Jackson, who, after leading the Bulls to their 6th NBA Championship in 8 years, was immediately let go after the 1998 season. He won the most coveted championship in the NBA six times and created a dynasty in the process. Still, those wins were not enough to secure his job. Now, I am in no way suggesting that Phil Jackson was not successful, and from what I have read, this guy flat-out did it the right way. I am just highlighting that even winning championships, even by doing it the right way and even achieving what most people would characterize as success, was still not enough to guarantee Phil Jackson's future with the Bulls. It will not secure yours either.

Here is some good news: This doesn't have to be your story. Living a successful life is within your control. In this book, you will learn that success is about your entire life, not merely one aspect. Success is about rhythm and living a life full of consistent, intentional actions that you will not regret down the road. Throughout this book, I will highlight many examples of people, teams, companies, and leaders who I believe are some of the most successful because of how they live their lives and build up others. Interestingly, these same people have created some of the winningest sports programs, are worth billions of dollars, have some of the strongest families, and have achieved great fame. But these accolades are all the byproducts of their consistent values and actions. They are the outcomes of how they live their lives on every level. Success for them is about becoming their best so that they can help others become better, too. Successful people are the ones who can go to bed every night, knowing that they have done all they can to become the best version of themselves. This guilt-free living allows them to develop lifelong relationships, create amazing companies, form tremendous teams, and genuinely live a life of joy, fulfillment, and success.

Living like this does not mean you settle or become complacent because you will still wake up every day seeking the dopamine hit to achieve. It is just that the hit that you are seeking is no longer concerned with material things or achievements outside of your control. Instead, the thrill of success is in knowing that you got better, helped people, and did all you could to win the day. This focus elevates every aspect of your life instead of distracting and luring you down the wrong path.

I am not a doctor, historian, or scientific guru. I am merely a guy who has been fortunate enough to collaborate with remarkable people, learn from some of the greatest teams, be impacted by great companies, and read about some of the most successful leaders, coaches, and teams this planet has ever seen. This book is designed to help you cut out the distractions in your life and focus on what matters so you, too, can be truly successful. It is designed to keep you from falling into the traps that deceive so many.

**THE THRILL OF SUCCESS IS IN KNOWING THAT YOU GOT BETTER, HELPED PEOPLE, AND DID ALL YOU COULD TO WIN THE DAY**

Throughout this book, I will highlight many of our societal distractions and the impact that I have seen them have on personal lives, relationships, health, and growth. Also, I will introduce a *Road to Success*, which includes the stages I believe are the common denominators for every successful person, team, and organization I have worked with or studied. When you learn the stages, apply them, and consistently follow them, you will become successful. You, too, can live without regret and leave a legacy that lasts beyond your years.

It is important to note that if you are merely reading this book so you can use these tools to get rich, win championships, or gain a title, then you should stop reading now because this isn't the book for you. The framework highlighted isn't some cheat code to help you ease through life. The *Road to Success* is the effort, the process, and the grind that must be made and followed each day from the time you wake up every morning until you lay your head down at night. There are no shortcuts.

## THE *ROAD TO SUCCESS*:

Stage 1: Know Your Identity
Stage 2: Change Your Thoughts
Stage 3: Take Action
Stage 4: Build Something That Lasts

If you consistently focus your attention and actions on these four stages, you will have a considerably high chance to obtain the wins, make the sales, achieve the accolades, garner the awards, and, most importantly, not sacrifice other aspects of your life to do so. But only if you have the discipline to live this way consistently.

It is also important to note that wanting to make a lot of money, leave a legacy, have a fantastic house, create an accomplished family, and gain a lot of influence are not bad things. In fact, these rewards should provide pleasure. If you cannot perform, don't win, or can't sell, then you won't have a job or business very long. Enjoying nice things is awesome; it just shouldn't be the goal. You must understand that though these outcomes may aid in living a satisfying life, they do not define your success. Rather, they are the byproduct of how you live your life.

I also want to point out that living on the **Road to Success** does not guarantee that you will win, but it does ensure that you will never lose. There is a significant difference between getting beat and losing. Sometimes, your opponent is just bigger, faster, and stronger. You might do everything right and still not be good enough to win in all situations. You can live on the **Road to Success** and have something outside of your control like death, disease, an accident, the weather, a recession, or an act of God swoop in and steal your victory. Though this still hurts, you can live without regrets because you know you gave your all and did everything possible. You just got beat. You can try again tomorrow.

> *THE ROAD TO SUCCESS* **DOES NOT GUARANTEE THAT YOU WILL WIN, BUT IT DOES ENSURE THAT YOU WILL NEVER LOSE**

Losing, on the other hand, is unacceptable. Unfortunately, way too many people lose. They lose in their relationships, they lose in their businesses, they lose in their finances, they lose the game, they lose in their health, in their marriages, and they lose as parents. Though most of all, these losers will convince themselves that they got beat, they didn't. They lost! They lost because they got distracted. They lost because they were fooled into believing that some thing, some title, some dollar amount, or some banner would provide meaning to their life. They lost because they allowed some excuse to prevent them from taking action. They lost because they were unprepared, not focused, missed something, or were not doing the right things.

If you read this book, put in the time to reflect on your values and priorities, and consistently apply the four stages on the **Road to Success,** I guarantee you will never lose another day. You might not always win, but it feels amazing knowing you gave it your all. It feels awesome to know you didn't miss out on important moments because you were distracted by the wrong things!

INTRODUCTION: ROAD TO SUCCESS
# CHAPTER 2: THE GREATS' DEFINITION OF SUCCESS

*"Peace of mind is a direct result of self-satisfaction in knowing you did your best to become the best you are capable of becoming."*
John Wooden

By now, you might think I'm on to something, or you might think I have no idea what matters. Either way, you are still reading, so let's look at a few people who I believe live lives of true success. I will highlight three remarkable people who not only have amazing families, are financially responsible, do things the right way, take care of their health, and invest in their marriages, but have also achieved accolades, titles, wealth, championships, and more. I will feature people who can honestly say that they give it their all, and because of how they live their lives, they will leave nothing to regret. I will tell their stories and let you be the judge of what is true and possible.

I challenge you to learn from them and perhaps imitate certain aspects of their lives. As you study them, you will notice some common themes. For one, their definition of success transcends their personal and professional lives. Secondly, it creates momentum and informs every aspect of their lives instead of luring them down the wrong path. Finally, their definition of success doesn't lead them to seek balance but instead create a rhythm to life so they can sustain productive activity over the entirety of their lives instead of burning out.

## WIZARD OF WESTWOOD, COACH JOHN WOODEN

Coach Wooden was a legendary Basketball coach for the UCLA Bruins from 1948 to 1975. He amassed a record of 620 wins and 147 losses over 27 years. He earned several records, including winning eighty-eight games in a row at one point and winning 10 National Championships, seven of those back-to-back (Arnett, 24). By societal measures, these achievements and accolades alone make him the greatest college basketball coach ever.

Interestingly, John Wooden would not have mentioned any of these things if you asked him to define success. Sure, he wanted to win, and he expected excellence, but success to him was having *"the peace of mind that is the direct result of self-satisfaction in knowing you did your best to become the best that you are capable of becoming."* (Arnett, 24) He wasn't concerned with the outside noise. He wasn't worried about what his competitors were doing, what the media said he should do, or how much money he had. Instead, he focused on becoming his best every day in every aspect of his life. He couldn't excel by bringing his best to the court and then neglecting his wife, his faith, his health, or his kids. At the same time, he couldn't just be a terrific husband at home and not give his best in his profession. Success for him was a daily focus and one that was never complete. He was never done growing, never done improving, and never done trying to be his best. Because of that, he excelled in every aspect of his life. Sure, his professional accolades speak for themselves. But what's even more impressive is that he was married to his high school sweetheart for 53 years, joined the US Navy during WWII and served until 1946, was a deep man of faith, was the father of 2 children, taught and coached his players to be men of character, and sought to be as healthy as he could be. (Arnett, 24)

John Wooden was not dependent on other people to make him successful. Nor was he so set in his ways that he was unwilling to change. He was constantly growing and improving as a person. John Wooden aimed to go to bed every night, knowing that he had done all that he could do that day to become a better person than he had been the day before. He aspired to rest peacefully, knowing that he treated his wife how she deserved to be treated and that their relationship was better today than it was before. He prioritized his health and ensured that he was doing the little things that could help him grow as old as possible and be as effective as possible for as long as possible. Coach Wooden focused on his players and ensured they were getting the best version of him so he could lead and mentor them to be their best. He was committed to being fully present when he was with his children. And when it came to his faith, it was his desire that «If he were ever prosecuted for his religion, that there would be enough evidence to convict him." The bottom line is that John Wooden believed his success was entirely within his control, and he was not concerned with the outside noise that could have easily distracted him. (Arnett, 24)

For John Wooden, success was not a distraction; it brought clarity, fulfillment, and energized him to keep going. Being his best empowered him throughout his entire day and in every aspect of his life. Living to always be your best informs you when you are out of whack, stressed, or in need of rest. It keeps you focused on priorities and ensures that you are productive instead of merely busy.

Because John Wooden was concerned with his character, his thoughts, his actions, and how he treated people, he was not deceived by all the pressure that distracts so many in his profession. Some could argue that he wasn't under as much pressure as coaches are today or that it was easier back in his day. However, I have learned that all struggles are relative. Not bigger, not greater, or easier, just relative. John Wooden had pressures and issues that made his job extremely challenging. However, his focus was to do his very best and be his very best in all situations and opportunities. He was successful if he got to the end of the day with the peace of mind, knowing that he did all he could to become his best self.

I don't care what generation you come from or what profession you've chosen; this concept of success plays everywhere. It works regardless of if you're old, young, male, or female. It works if you are in technology, lumber, construction, real estate, banking, education, or politics. It works everywhere because this truth is universal. Your consistent and selfless actions and how you think will create opportunities that can lead to success in any field. For Coach Wooden, it was basketball. What will it be for you?

This way of life is not easy, but it is simple, and that's the beauty. We all can do it. You can discover your best self and ensure that you keep getting better. When you get better, your relationships, your health, and your business get better because better people make better people.

**YOUR CONSISTENT AND SELFLESS ACTIONS AND HOW YOU THINK WILL CREATE OPPORTUNITIES THAT CAN LEAD TO SUCCESS IN ANY FIELD.**

## WHAT CHARACTERISTICS, BEHAVIORS, AND ACTIONS DO YOU DISPLAY WHEN YOU ARE AT YOUR BEST?

## WHAT CHARACTERISTICS, BEHAVIORS, AND ACTIONS DO YOU DISPLAY WHEN YOU ARE AT YOUR WORST?

## ASK 2-3 PEOPLE CLOSE TO YOU WHAT CHARACTERISTICS, BEHAVIORS, AND ACTIONS THEY SEE FROM YOU WHEN YOU ARE AT YOUR BEST AND WORST. SEEK FEEDBACK FROM THOSE YOU TRUST AND WHO WILL BE BRUTALLY HONEST. WRITE DOWN WHAT YOU HEARD.

## SIR RICHARD BRANSON

Maybe coaching isn't your thing, and though John Wooden's life is impressive, you don't relate to it. In that case, let us look at the life of Sir Richard Branson. This is a man who dropped out of school at the age of fifteen, started his first business at the age of sixteen, became the founder of Virgin a couple of years later, and now owns forty companies in industries including music, cell phones, planes, trains, and cruise lines. He is worth several billion dollars, influences healthcare politics, and is even into intergalactic travel. He has thousands of employees, has been Knighted by England, participates in many philanthropic ventures, is an adventurer who holds world records for balloon travel, has been married to the same woman since 1989, and is the father of three children. (Haden, 2023) This man, on paper, is as accomplished as they come. Yet, like John Wooden, he would not mention any of this when defining success. Sure, he wants his businesses to flourish, expects to make a lot of money, and wants an amazing family, but he believes his happiness measures true success. He believes that if you are unhappy, you might be embracing conflicting definitions of professional and personal success. Sir Richard Branson believes that your professional and personal success must align, and when this is the case, you *will* be happy. (Haden, 2023) By living this way, your professional goals are feeding your personal goals, and vice versa. Branson can maximize his time and effort because he is not competing against himself. He is not at home thinking about work, and he is not at work thinking of all that he is missing at home. Coincidentally, the happier he is, typically, the more wealth, greater impact, better performance, and more loving relationships he creates. His outcomes, the ones so many of us are chasing, are merely the byproducts of his happiness. (Haden, 2023)

Just like John Wooden, Richard Branson is not distracted by superficial achievements. Nor is he so limited in thinking that he's only trying to succeed in one area of his life. He knows that money can provide the opportunity to do many things, but if all he has is money, then he is the poorest person in the world. What's the point of getting to the end of your life and dying with a ton of money and no relationships? Who cares how many businesses you have or how far you go if you don't have people sharing your journey?

Seeking happiness allows Richard Branson to be successful every day and in every moment of his life. Happiness allows him to celebrate his wins and failures because if you are not failing at times, you aren't trying hard enough and aren't growing. Happiness isn't some scarce resource that only money can buy, or that is only reserved for a select few. Happiness is available to all of us, and if you want to adopt this view of success, seek it by following Scottish

> **WHAT'S THE POINT OF GETTING TO THE END OF YOUR LIFE AND DYING WITH A TON OF MONEY AND NO RELATIONSHIPS?**

Biographer Alexander Chalmers's definition of happiness. Chalmers said, "To be happy, you need something to love, something to do, and something to look forward to." This applies to all areas of your life. Finding something you love at work, at home, and everywhere else you spend time will bring you joy. Accomplishing productive things within your career, finances, hobbies, and relationships will provide you fulfillment. Finally, having goals within multiple areas of your life will supply you with motivation. This type of living encourages us, keeps us focused, and provides happiness that overflows into every area of our lives.

# IN YOUR PERSONAL LIFE
## WHAT DO YOU LOVE?

## WHAT ARE YOUR RESPONSIBILITIES?

## WHAT ARE YOU LOOKING FORWARD TO?

# IN YOUR PROFESSIONAL LIFE
## WHAT DO YOU LOVE?



## WHAT ARE YOUR RESPONSIBILITIES?



## WHAT ARE YOU LOOKING FORWARD TO?



## IF YOU STRUGGLE WITH ANY OF THESE ANSWERS, MAKE A PLAN RIGHT NOW TO FIND OR DO MORE OF WHAT YOU LOVE, TAKE ON A NEW RESPONSIBILITY, AND/OR PLAN SOMETHING YOU CAN LOOK FORWARD TO. WHEN CREATING A PLAN, IT MUST BE CLEAR AND DETAILED. INCLUDE THE PLACE, THE TIME, WHO WILL BE THERE, AND WHAT NEEDS TO BE ACCOMPLISHED.



## DEREK JETER

If John Wooden and Richard Branson are not enough to convince you that success is more than the material things of this world, I will now highlight Derek Jeter, the former starting shortstop for the New York Yankees. Jeter had one of the greatest MLB careers of all time. He played his entire 20-year career with the Yankees, won five World Series, five Gold Gloves, and five Silver Slugger Awards. He also holds many Yankee Records, was elected to the Major League Baseball Hall of Fame, and had his number retired by the Yankees. (Brockmeyer, 04)

After playing, Jeter became a partial owner/CEO of the Miami Marlins, engages in many other businesses, is a color commentator for professional baseball, has been married since 2012, and is the father of four children (Brockmeyer, 04). Yet, like John Wooden and Richard Branson, Derek Jeter knows that success is not something you do; it's something you are. His success depends on his character, work ethic, effort, and mindset to be the best in everything he does.

Success isn't something he does occasionally, only when others are watching, or is something that he will ever fully achieve. Success is something he is all day, every day. It is how he operates; his mindset transfers throughout all areas of his life. It worked in baseball, in all he has done since, in his personal life, and will work in all he decides to do in the future.

The same is true for you. Either you are a success, or you aren't. Either you are doing things to improve yourself and those around you, or you're not. There is no middle ground. Derek Jeter knows this. Because he never stops pursuing success, he always gets better. His relationships get better, his parenting gets better, his play gets better, his health gets better, and his life gets better. Success is always within his control, allowing his transition out of his sport to be peaceful instead of providing a significant sense of loss, grief, or other negative emotions that plague so many athletes after retirement. (Scipioni, 2020)

> **EITHER YOU ARE DOING THINGS TO IMPROVE YOURSELF AND THOSE AROUND YOU, OR YOU'RE NOT. THERE IS NO MIDDLE GROUND.**

Stop trying to achieve success and start being a success. Focus on what you can control and then do the work to make yourself better every day because this life pursuit will remove regret and lead to greatness in every aspect of your life.

## WHAT EVERYDAY ACTIONS DO YOU HAVE FULL CONTROL OVER?

INTRODUCTION: ROAD TO SUCCESS
# CHAPTER 3: HOW TO DEFINE YOUR SUCCESS

*Successful people do what unsuccessful people are not willing to do. Don't wish it were easier; wish you were better.*
**Jim Rohn**
*Do not pray for easy lives; pray to be stronger men. Do not pray for tasks equal to your powers. Pray for power equal to your tasks."*
**John F. Kennedy**

I grew up on a large farm in Southern Indiana. My mom and dad, two brothers and one sister, and I all lived in a small two-bedroom, one-bath house we loved. We built forts, went fishing, had a horse trough for a swimming pool, played basketball every day, hit rocks with our baseball bats, rode motorcycles, shared a sandbox with some stray cats, had cows, horses, pigs, dogs, and a goose that was more of guard dog than a bird. We played every sport our community offered, attended church every Sunday, and even found time to go to school.

As a child, I never really remember talking much about success. We just saw it! Farming is highly demanding work. There is always something that needs to be done, and those who live on the farm are the ones who must do it. It doesn't matter if you are tired or want to; the work must be done. I witnessed every day how my dad just did the work. He would be up before sunrise, tending to the cows, feeding horses, discing the fields, planting crops, fertilizing the plants, and harvesting the corn, beans, and alfalfa. As a farmer, my dad even had to play veterinarian as he would give the livestock medicine and help deliver calves. In the winter, he would have to go out multiple times during the day to break up the ice accumulating in the animals' troughs so they had something to drink. Farming is a never-ending job that requires grit, consistency, and exhausting work. What's incredible is that I never heard my dad complain. I never saw him upset that he had to get up early. I don't remember him ever missing a day, regardless if he felt terrible, was tired, or had something better to do. He never gave up or had an excuse; he just got the job done!

When I was in the third grade, I saw his grit and determination displayed again when we, unfortunately, lost our farm, and my dad had to do something to provide for our family. Now that I am an adult, I can imagine how stressed, frustrated, and afraid my dad must have been, knowing he needed to provide. But I never witnessed it. I never saw any of this. He just figured it out. He got to work, found us a new home, started his own construction business, and once again put food on the table. It was as if nothing happened. He never skipped a beat. I didn't realize it then, but I witnessed someone practicing success. I never heard my dad talk

**WHEN YOU HAVE SOMEONE SO INFLUENTIAL SPEAKING LIFE INTO YOU DAY AFTER DAY, AFTER A WHILE, YOU BEGIN TO BELIEVE IT.**

about money, and I never heard him fixate on a title. I just saw him work. I saw how he controlled his emotions, protected us, kept us from worrying, and one byproduct of his efforts was a fantastic childhood for me.

At the same time, we had the mom of all moms! The mom who taught us to love, who ensured we were cared for, and who was there to develop us into people of empathy. Our father absolutely loved us; he cared deeply for us and would do anything for us, but he would even say that our mom taught us to love. We knew that our mom would love us no matter what, and this gave us the confidence to try anything in the world. She spoke life into us and told us we could do anything. She didn't lie to us or plant false hope. She challenged us and taught us to believe in ourselves. When you have someone so influential speaking life into you day after day, after a while, you begin to believe it. With this type of unconditional love, my siblings and I had the support to do new things. We had the confidence to go after our dreams because we knew we would always be loved, no matter what. What a great safety net! We all learned how to work and acquired the grit necessary to push through life's challenges. Most importantly, though, we learned to do it with love. We saw how our mom treated and interacted with us, impacting how we treated others. We cared for, helped, and loved those around us. You better believe that we wanted to win and be our best, but not at the expense of hurting others. Not at the expense of using or abusing those around us. We all wanted to be great stewards of the gifts that our parents provided for us.

My parents didn't discuss grades or offer us incentives if we played hard or scored in a game. They didn't attempt to relive their life through ours, demand that we dominate, or chastise us when we didn't. Yes, they wanted us to have good grades, wanted us to win, and hoped that we would perform. But our parents only focused on our behaviors. They challenged us to give our best and put in the work, and if we did, our grades took care of themselves, we often won, and most certainly, our performance improved. When we did win, my parents expected us to do it with class. We were taught never to gloat or rub it in; we didn't embarrass the opponent or make fun of those less talented. In our family's version of success, you won when you did things the right way or you weren't a winner at all. This went for school, while we were with our friends, and when we were at church or just running around our small town. Our character was way more important to our parents than any accolade we earned.

Don't think there wasn't discipline in the house for a second. We knew the expectations and how we were supposed to behave, and if we didn't, it was addressed. We were not spanked, we weren't belittled, we were parented. We were praised when we were doing things right and redirected when we weren't. We were always encouraged to find ways to be better, think better, behave better, and treat others better.

From this parenting, I realized that I usually won when I gave my best, worked as hard as I could, and did things the right way, regardless of who was watching. I usually got good grades and rarely had discipline issues. When I gave my best, I typically made people around me feel important. But, when I didn't work my hardest, sought shortcuts, or did the wrong thing because I knew no one was watching, I usually lost or was left with a ton of regret. If I did win but did so by cheating, I felt so disappointed with myself and was left with worry and fear that someone would find out. Such a false version of success is exhausting.

I have found that the feeling of guilt tends to overpower the feeling of winning. Guilt or regret is more destructive than winning is productive. For instance, I was fortunate to play

## GUILT OR REGRET IS MORE DESTRUCTIVE THAN WINNING IS PRODUCTIVE.

college baseball for Purdue University; it was something I had worked hard to accomplish and a fantastic experience I will cherish forever. While there, I worked my butt off, I was positive, I was always up for taking more hacks in the cage, I put in extra work, and I was willing to do whatever the team needed. But, looking back, I regret that my confidence wasn't higher. I regret that I doubted my abilities. I regret that I compared myself to others. I regret that in the first three years, I tried so hard to please my coach instead of just playing the game I loved. I regret trying to be a player I wasn't. These actions made me a passive player who wouldn't take chances in a game because he was afraid to fail. It wasn't until my last year of playing that I realized I couldn't please everyone; I could only be who I was, and I needed to play the game the best way I could. If it wasn't good enough, then it wasn't. But at least I would find out how good I was and play the game the only way I knew how. Interestingly, I played more when I had this mindset; I had better at-bats, was less worried about pleasing others, and had much more fun. It didn't mean I played a lot because I didn't, but that last year was a season of no regrets.

My last season was my best because I finally felt free. Unfortunately, those first three years of college left a regretful feeling in my mind because I knew that it was me, not the game, not the coach, and not the opponent that kept me from being my best. It was my mindset, and this memory stinks because I can't go back and fix those three years. We can't redo life's moments or seasons. We must maximize the now to ensure we don't create new regrets in the future.

Guilt and regret stem from our behaviors, thinking, and how we hurt those close to us. When we do anything but be our best for those around us, we set ourselves up for a life of regret. But, when we give our best and do all we can, regardless of how we feel, when we go after our dreams, when we are okay to look silly and flat-out love those around us, there is no regret. There is immense joy because we know we gave all we could.

Yes, I have regrets. I don't like them and don't want to experience them again. I have lied, cheated, and failed to give my best. I have been distracted, sought personal glory, and done things so others would praise me. I have neglected people I love so I could win. I have said hurtful things that I wish I could take back, and I have passed on saying helpful things that I wish I had said. I have stayed in un-healthy relationships for too long and ended good relationships I should have appreciated more. There have been dreams I've gone after but others I let slip by. There have been phone calls I made that hurt and other calls I wish I had made to people who are no longer with us. I am done adding to my regrets. I no longer want to go to bed at night wishing I had done things differently, been more fo-cused, or that I had done what I said I was going to do. I want to go to bed each night, knowing I did all I could to be the best version of myself. This is where true peace and fulfillment rest.

Living without regret doesn't mean we won't mess up, and it doesn't guarantee that we will win. Seeking to live without regret means we take complete control of the process. When I am at my best, I'm not attempting to control the outside influences; I am controlling my actions, behaviors, and responses to what life throws my way. Seeking to live a life without regret is ongoing and never finished, and it gives me a purpose to live for every day. I don't want to wait to do the things on my bucket list. I want to live life to the full now while

**SEEKING TO LIVE WITHOUT REGRET MEANS WE TAKE COMPLETE CONTROL OF THE PROCESS.**

I can. Living with no regrets allows me to celebrate the challenges, the work, the love, the fun, and the growth, yet not obsess over the performance, be a glutton for titles, or be consumed by the wins. I can live in such a way that I find joy, happiness, and peace of mind, knowing that I did all I could to become the best I could be. Living this way allows my accomplishments to be byproducts of my way of life. My relationships are strong because of how I live my life. My business is strong because of how I live my life. My faith is strong because of how I live my life. My marriage is awesome because of how I live my life. My family is amazing because of how I live my life. Whatever legacy I leave will be because of how I lived my life!

I haven't accomplished all the feats of John Wooden, Richard Branson, Derek Jeter, or the other amazing people in this book. However, I do live a life of happiness, a life full of blessings, and it is because I am not distracted by someone else's success. I am empowered by my success, which is built from knowing myself, thinking differently, taking action, and working to build something that lasts.

When you adopt a similar mindset and belief, you'll find that you'll be less stressed, happier, less worried, and more fulfilled. You'll find less anguish and more joy, and you'll start doing the things you love now instead of waiting until it is too late.

Before you read any further, you must figure out where you're going. You must know what success looks like to you, ensure it is entirely within your control, transcends your personal and professional lives, and isn't fixated on the outcome.

So, start here. Answer the questions below and begin to create your unique definition of success.

## WHAT BEHAVIORS AND ACTIONS LEAD YOU TO A FEELING OF PRIDE OR JOY WHEN YOU ARE EXHIBITING THEM?

## WHAT BRINGS A SENSE OF PURPOSE TO YOUR LIFE BEYOND PROFESSIONAL GOALS?

# WHAT BRINGS YOU A SENSE OF FULFILLMENT DAILY?

# WHO ARE SOME SUCCESSFUL PEOPLE IN YOUR LIFE?

# WHAT BEHAVIORS AND ACTIONS DO YOU SEE THEM EXHIBIT ON A REGULAR BASIS?

# ASK A FEW OF THEM THEIR DEFINITION OF SUCCESS AND WRITE THEM HERE.

# MAYBE IT IS THE SAME, OR MAYBE IT HAS CHANGED OR EVOLVED. EITHER WAY, WRITE YOUR DEFINITION OF SUCCESS AGAIN.

To create a community committed to helping us all become our best, we made the Distracted by Success Facebook Group below. This community is a place to share our best practices, learn from others seeking to become their best and be held accountable for doing what we should. To best help you become the person you want to be, we would love it if you joined our group and shared your definition of success, read and comment on those who are also a part of the group, and encourage us all to improve. We all know what we are supposed to do; often, we need a community to keep us on the right path.  Please follow the link below and request to join our community. Then, share your definition of success.

www.facebook.com/groups/distractedbysuccess/

ROAD TO SUCCESS
# STAGE ONE: KNOW YOUR IDENTITY

STAGE ONE: KNOW YOUR IDENTITY
# CHAPTER 4: DISTRACTED IDENTITY

*"Be yourself; everyone else is already taken."*
**Oscar Wilde**

Living without regret, being happy, or living with peace of mind knowing that you did all you could to be your best sounds nice, but how do you do this? How do you ensure you are not distracted by success but instead focused, productive, and living a significant life?

I believe it comes down to following the **Road to Success Framework**, the stages or ways of life that I have found to be common denominators among the truly successful people, teams, organizations, families, and companies I have worked with or studied. When you know the stages of the framework and live by them, you're guaranteed to live a life without regret. You will get to the end of your day, week, month, year, or life and not wish you had done something different. You will find out just how great you can be.

This first step is to know your identity.

# WHO ARE YOU?

## WHAT ARE THE FIRST WORDS OR PHRASES YOU USE TO DESCRIBE WHO YOU ARE?

Unfortunately, many of us have never taken the time to reflect on who we are, let alone take the time to write it down. So, not surprisingly, many of us don't really know ourselves. If this is the case for you, then you probably don't have an idea of how you are supposed to respond or how you should behave based on the circumstances life throws your way. You may be happy in one moment and extremely sad in the next. You may be pleasant to some people and then mean to someone else. You may appear to be the most loyal person in the world to some and, simultaneously, the least trustworthy person to others. You might seem like you have it all together and then be ready to fall apart at the first sign of trouble. Such a lack of authenticity can destroy relationships, lives, and professions. Your goal should be consistency. Being the same person regardless of the situation or who you are with. But to do this, you must know for certain who you are.

When you have no idea who you are, your identity becomes dependent on being liked. It's about fitting in and doing whatever it takes for people to like you. When this is true, you will do whatever with whomever and wherever, so long as people like you. Don't get me wrong; I want to be liked, have friends, and have people say good things about me. Because if I didn't, there would be no chance of me having any satisfying relationships. But things become destructive when my identity is dependent upon the opinions of others.

Just think about the crazy, destructive things you've done because you wanted to fit in. Maybe it was your first drink of alcohol, your first cigarette, or your first drug. You knew it wasn't right but did it anyway because you wanted to fit in.

Think of what you've been willing to do to try and make that guy or girl like you. Some might dress provocatively or do things sexually they aren't ready for. Many people will change how they look, the size of their breasts, the shape of their nose, or the thickness of their lips, all to be liked. Recall the number of individuals you thought had solid morals, yet when they got involved with the wrong group of friends, it was as if all their ethics were thrown out the window. They drank too much, flirted, or worse, cheated on their partner, and most certainly did things they regretted the next morning. Why? Because they wanted to fit in, they fell victim to peer pressure and did whatever it took to be liked.

Talk to almost any middle school student, and you're likely to hear stories of classmates claiming to be cats, dogs, or even Furby's (a hamster-looking toy with big eyes.) Though I am not a psychologist and don't have any medical studies to back this up, I bet these behaviors are all strongly related to a need to be liked. These young students are so desperate to fit in somewhere that they will do anything to make that happen, even if that means identifying as an animal or a toy.

Also, think of the people you work with who will never make a decision, have an opinion, or hold someone accountable because they don't want to upset or offend anyone. Think of those who execute unethical or immoral demands made by their boss simply because they want to gain favor or appear as a team player. Some husbands or wives will do whatever they can to appease their spouse, always accommodate, and never raise concerns or challenge their spouse to improve because they don't want to upset their partner. Thus, the relationship grows stale, and destructive behaviors begin.

success, leadership, relationships, and our identity are not about being liked but about being respected. Don't get me wrong; wanting to be liked isn't the problem. However, you must realize that relationships aren't built on always agreeing. They are built on respect. It is about valuing yourself, valuing others, valuing the institution, and living in such a way that garners the same from everyone else. When we live like this, people tend to like us. Strong relationships become the byproduct, not the focus.

Unfortunately, with today's social media culture, the need to be liked is becoming even more prevalent. We post on Facebook, Instagram, TikTok, Snapchat, and Twitter so that everyone can see our lives, and then we desperately hope they click that "LIKE" button. When they don't, and we aren't solid in knowing our identity, self-doubt begins to creep in. We start to wonder what is wrong with us and why they don't like us. We start comparing ourselves to others, wondering why they get likes and we don't, and this need to be noticed can cause us to post whatever it takes to get likes. We may post negative and demeaning texts like those that dominate our feeds. We may post gossip and hurtful things about people so others will read, comment, and reshare our negativity. Girls and women will post seductive pictures or videos to gain the attention they so desire. All the while, our need to be liked is destroying our lives, relationships, and reputations. All the while, these distractions create a life we will one day regret.

The need to be liked is everywhere. Just think of famous actors, musicians, or artists. These highly talented people are loved because of their incredible talents in acting, singing, and creating beautiful pieces of art. The love they receive from fans encourages the artists to continue creating more content. So, they return to work and put **WHO ARE YOU?** the same amount of time, effort, and energy into a new project. But sometimes the new work doesn't resonate with their fans, or people may not get it and, therefore, don't like or buy it. Because not as many people enjoy their new movie, song, or creation, self-doubt creeps in. These amazing people become depressed or lost because they don't feel liked, and their self-worth is dependent upon others' opinions. This self-doubt can cause many to turn to destructive behaviors to numb the pain. Such as drugs, alcohol, sex, or some other addiction, to escape their loss of identity.

Let me ask the question again: Who are you?

## HOW ARE YOU LIVING AND BEHAVING IN SUCH A WAY TO GET "LIKES"?

## WHEN DO YOU AVOID DIFFICULT CONVERSATIONS BECAUSE YOU DON'T WANT TO UPSET SOMEONE OR HURT FEELINGS?

## HOW DOES YOUR BEHAVIOR CHANGE IN DIFFERENT SETTINGS?

Are you one person at work, another at home, and yet another when you are with your friends, by yourself, or at church?

If your behaviors change based on your setting, then you don't know who you are. Whether you want to admit it or not, you are desperately attempting to impress and be liked. Your lack of authenticity will prevent you from being truly successful. It's time to figure out who you are!

Maybe you're thinking this isn't you. Perhaps you know exactly who you are. Maybe you immediately began rattling off things like you are a mom, dad, husband, or wife. You are a teacher, coach, doctor, or lawyer: a soldier, an athlete, a CEO, or a pastor. But here's the issue: this is not *who* you are. These are your titles or your profession. Though these things are important, you set yourself up for failure and a life of regret when you wrap your identity around your career or titles. Think of all the people you have seen who have become lost, depressed, or a trainwreck once their career is over. Think of the destruction that can be caused when someone is consumed or obsessed with their title and then it is stripped away. Think of those who become lost once their children move away from home.

I have seen countless people dedicate their entire lives to their careers. They sacrifice everything because they believe they are the company's cornerstone. They think the company will crumble without them, or the team will cease to exist. But whether you believe it or not, work will still get done regardless if you show up. When you step down, leave, or are no longer in your position, there will be someone to fill your void. There will be many eager for the shot to take your place.

When legendary college football coach Nick Saban stepped down as the Head Coach for the University of Alabama, his seat remained vacant for two days. This guy is the greatest college football coach the country has ever seen regarding wins, national championships, and having first-round NFL draft picks, yet his seat sat empty for only two days. I share this to highlight that another person can quickly fill any position. Your titles will one day belong to someone else, but there will never be another you. No one will ever have your calling or be a better you.

It is so common for athletes to struggle when transitioning out of their sport because they mainly see themselves as "a gymnast," "a dancer," "a linebacker," or "a shortstop." I know because I experienced it, and I've seen it over and over. Athletes believe their ability to spin a football, run a quick 40-yard dash, bench press 400 pounds, flip a vault, or perform a quadruple pirouette makes them unique and special. They believe it is what their life is all about and what makes up their identity. Unfortunately, their athletic career will end, and when it does, they no longer know who they are. Once athletes are done playing, many feel sorry for themselves and are lost. They turn to alcohol and drugs, become depressed, and end up taking some random job because they don't believe they have any value left. Don't misunderstand me; flipping vaults, being fast, and crushing home runs are all super cool, but that's not what made these exceptional athletes unique. They are unique because they possess grit, tenacity, and discipline. They are unique because they are coachable, humble, enthusiastic, willing to fail, and mentally tougher than most in the world. It's these characteristics that make them who they are; it's these values that are wanted and desired in all professions and life titles.

Unfortunately, Psychologists N.B Suambulova and Professor Paul Wylleman discovered that it takes two years for most professional athletes to truly transition out of their sport, and one athlete in five experiences a true crisis once they leave their sport. This time of crisis includes depression, anxiety, physical pain, and loss of purpose and self-worth. Twenty percent of athletes, some of the hardest working, most loyal, most enthusiastic, and coachable people in the world, struggle to transition because they have no idea who they are without their role as athletes. (Wylleman and Lavallee, 2021)

At the same time, many athletes and professionals fall in love with the fame, power, glitz, and glamour that come with stardom. How could you not? To have people chanting your name, hanging on to your every Tweet, worshiping your every song, and memorializing your every play would feel great. These very bright lights distract many. It gives them a false sense of power and a sense of entitlement that they can do whatever they want with no repercussions. Just recall the number of celebrities, politicians, and athletes whose lives, reputations, and families have been destroyed because of their questionable behaviors. Like Tiger Woods, the greatest golfer of all time and the player who did more for the sport of golf than anyone, yet ended up crushing his reputation, ruining his marriage, and hurting his family due to all his extramarital affairs. Then there's Matt Lauer, who was one of the most prominent faces on television and the pride of NBC, who eventually had his career, reputation, and marriage destroyed because he sexually harassed and had inappropriate sexual relations with multiple women at work. Bill Cosby, who at one point was the highest-paid actor in the world and was adored by fans, lost it all and spent several years in prison once he was found guilty of rape, battery, and sexual misconduct.

How does this happen? I don't know these men or have any evidence that this is true, but I don't think they were born evil. I do not believe that any of these men got into their roles or became as great as they were so they could one day destroy people's lives, their own reputations, families, and marriages. I believe they got distracted and lost sight of who they were. They fell in love with power and thought people worshipped them rather than the seat they sat in. They began wrapping their identity around the lights, money, and supremacy instead of upholding the values that brought them success in the first place. They started making one small immoral or unethical behavior at a time. These minor violations weren't noticed or corrected until they had gone on for so long and became so bad that these celebrities were eventually exposed. Tiger Woods, Matt Lauer, and Bill Cosby had become so distracted that they eventually became someone so removed from who they once were or believed they were that destruction was all that could happen.

You and I are not immune to these destructive mistakes. Think of the number of affairs you've seen in the workplace. Most guilty parties would claim to be honest, loyal, and loving people. Most guilty parties would claim that they didn't set out to have an affair and couldn't even tell you how it happened. Because it happened one small step at a time. One little unethical violation after another, most not even noticeable, until one day, it became a full-fledged affair.

Having your identity wrapped up in what you do doesn't necessarily mean that your marriage will end, that you will become addicted to drugs, that you will have a dysfunctional family, or that you will destroy your reputation. But not knowing who you are can also prevent you from going after your dreams, keep you in a job you no longer enjoy, and stop you from living the life you want. I have worked with coaches, teachers, lawyers, doctors, mothers, and fathers who believe the profession they originally picked is where they are destined to be stuck. People feel their life is what it is: shuttling kids from place to place, designing a defense, or diagnosing injuries. They miss that they already are executing high-demand skills like organizing an entire family schedule, leading hundreds of people toward a mission, and making life-altering decisions on a second's notice. Their false sense of identity causes them to settle. They settle for a career that they no longer love. They settle for a job because it is comfortable, stable, and just blah. Yet if they saw themselves for who they really were, if their gifts resided in their values and character, they would see they could do whatever they dreamed of. They could surpass goals, fail, learn, grow, and live a fantastic life because they didn't believe the lie about who they really are.

## ONCE AGAIN, WHO ARE YOU?

## WHAT VALUES, BEHAVIORS, AND CHARACTERISTICS BEST DEFINE WHO YOU ARE?

Your identity must be rooted in your values. You must define yourself based on your behaviors, as your values remind you of who you are, regardless of what happens to you or around you. They keep you grounded and allow you to easily transition into any stage of life. Your identity becomes a plug-and-play

**YOUR IDENTITY MUST BE ROOTED IN YOUR VALUES.**

system. It doesn't matter where you are, who you are with, or what is happening in your life; you are the same authentic person striving to improve. You aren't distracted by the title, power, money, glitz, or glamour. You aren't concerned with being liked or attempting to please everyone. You don't feel a sense of entitlement or believe you are immune to wrongdoings. You are just you. Held accountable by your values. Which humbles you and allows you to live a life of no regrets.

DISTRACTED IDENTITY

STAGE ONE: KNOW YOUR IDENTITY
# CHAPTER 5: THE GREATS' IDENTITY

*I'd be pretty dumb if, all of a sudden, I started being something I'm not.*
**Yogi Berra**

In the movie, "The Greatest Showman," artist Keala Brown sings the song "This is Me," which starts off expressing the fears that so many of us face when trying to be ourselves. She mentions that no one wants to see our broken parts, that we should run away, and that no one will love you as you are. Unfortunately, this is how so many of us live. We live as if we aren't unique; we live as if God may have made a mistake. But that is never the case; God doesn't say oops. As Keala Brown goes on to sing, "I am brave, I am bruised, I am who I'm meant to be, this is me." When you know and love who you are, "You will become a warrior reaching for the sun!"

I encourage you to watch the movie and listen to that song if you haven't already. They hit the importance of identity on the head. Too many of us get caught up in what others think of us, trying to be someone we're not, feeling as if our past somehow dictates our future, that we fail to live a life of success. It doesn't have to be like this. When you look at the greats, you'll realize that they aren't trying to impress anyone, aren't holding onto some title, and don't get hung up on their failures. They know who they are and are constantly seeking to improve that person.

When you look at John Wooden, he was not just some basketball coach. He wasn't just a husband, father, or some guy who attended church. No, he was a man of faith; he was a man who put others first. He was a man who did what he said, treated people with respect, was organized, prepared, and always willing to go the extra mile to help someone in need. (Arnett, 24) John Wooden wasn't distracted by winning games, hoisting championship banners, or being the center of attention. He wasn't trying to be liked or concerned with what people thought of him. Instead, he challenged himself and those around him by stating, "Be more concerned with your character than your reputation because your character is who you really are, while your reputation is merely what others think you are."

With this as his focus, it didn't matter where John Wooden was, who he was with, how his team performed, or what the world threw at him. He was always John Wooden. No matter the circumstance, he faced each situation with his values intact: to do what he said, treat people with respect, be organized and prepared, and always be willing to go the extra mile to help someone in need. Period. This was his identity. This was how he measured success. He was just himself and always striving to improve. As he got better, everything else around him got better. His relationships were better, his marriage was better, his days were better, his teams were better, and his life was just better.

The greats, the ones who build amazing relationships, are happy, don't sacrifice their morals for achievements, and know precisely who they are; live their values no matter where they are,

**IT'S MY WIFE'S VALUES THAT MAKE HER SO UNIQUE AND SUCCESSFUL.**

who they are with, or what happens in their life. It's this consistency that leads to their success. For instance, my wife, Kerry, is easily the most incredible person I have ever known. Why? Because she knows exactly who she is, and her authenticity is beautiful. She doesn't make millions of dollars or pose on the cover of magazines (though she could because she is stunning). She doesn't have millions of followers on social media or run a multi-billion-dollar company. She isn't stuck in a high-paying job she hates and doesn't hold a political seat of power. She is a woman who loves God, adores her children, does what she says she is going to do, cares for all those near her, strives to be a better person today than she was yesterday, is as mentally tough as anyone I've met, loves me with all her heart (which that alone makes her the most amazing person ever), is as loyal as they get, will own her mistakes, and makes our home a little better every day. It's my wife's values that make her so unique and successful. Her authenticity is so attractive and from where everything in our life grows. Because she lives her values daily, she doesn't waste time on pointless things, deal in drama, or ruminate over the past. She doesn't allow her fears to prevent her from trying something new and treats the beggar just as kindly as the CEO.

When you see her, you are in awe because she always brings the same focus, determination, and care to each project. It doesn't matter if she's volunteering at our church, creating some form of social media marketing for our business, exercising, or learning to make sourdough bread; she owns it. Seeing her interact with our children is just some kind of awesome because she cares so much. She isn't a helicopter parent hovering over their every move; she is just involved. She knows what's going on in our children's lives, what they love, where they are struggling, and then guides them to improve. She challenges them, holds them accountable, and flat-out loves them more than I think anyone could love. It's these behaviors that have made our kids so awesome and our family so incredible. My wife is impressive because she knows who she is and brings that same identity no matter where she is.

Her family, marriage, friends, career, and life are the byproducts of who she is. They are the outcomes of my wife consistently living up to her values. It is what can happen to you if you were to truly know who you are and seek to live your values each day. My wife will tell you that she isn't perfect and never claims to be, but she is authentic, and I don't know if there's anything more beautiful than a person who loves who they are. I don't know that there is anything more powerful than a person who is confident and focused enough to be their best self regardless of the pressures and distractions surrounding them because this type of person is sure to live a life of no regrets.

The greats have learned that living by their values, not their title, achievements, or performance, brings humility. They are grounded in what matters and not distracted by the material things of this world. This focus allows them to succeed in every aspect of life.

To highlight this aspect one final time, before we learn how to discover our identity, I want to share a story I read several years ago by a former United States Under Secretary of Defense.

> He took his place on the stage and began talking, sharing his prepared remarks with the audience. He paused to take a sip of coffee from the Styrofoam cup he'd brought on stage with him. He took another sip, looked down at the cup, and smiled.
>
> "You know," he said, interrupting his own speech, "I spoke here last year. I presented at this same conference on the same stage. But last year, I was still an Under Secretary," he said. "I flew here in business class, and when I landed, there was someone waiting for me at the airport to take me to my hotel. Upon arriving at my hotel," he continued, "there was someone else waiting for me. They had already checked me into the hotel, so they handed me my key and escorted me to my room. The next morning, when I came down again, someone was waiting for me in the lobby to drive me to the same venue we are in today. I was taken through a back entrance, shown to the greenroom, and handed a cup of coffee in a beautiful ceramic cup."
>
> "But this year, as I stand here to speak to you, I am no longer the Under Secretary," he continued. "I flew here by coach class, and when I arrived at the airport yesterday, no one was there to meet me. I took a taxi to the hotel, and when I got there, I checked myself in and went by myself to my room. This morning, I came down to the lobby and caught another taxi to come here. I went in the front door and found my way backstage. Once there, I asked one of the techs if there was any coffee. He pointed to a coffee machine on a table against the wall. So, I walked over and poured myself a cup of coffee

into this Styrofoam cup," he said as he raised the cup to show the audience.

"It occurs to me," he continued, "the ceramic cup they gave me last year… was never meant for me. It was meant for the position I held. I deserve a Styrofoam cup."

"This is the most important lesson I can impart to all of you," he offered. "All the perks, all the benefits and advantages you may get for the rank or position you hold, they aren't meant for you. They are meant for the role you fill. When you leave your role, which you will eventually do, they will give the ceramic cup to the person who replaces you. Because you only ever deserved a Styrofoam cup." (Marcus, 2018)

This is such a great story because it once again highlights that things, titles, and power don't matter. They will go away. Your values and your character will stand the test of time.

STAGE ONE: KNOW YOUR IDENTITY
# CHAPTER 6:
# HOW TO DISCOVER YOUR IDENTITY

*Character is like a tree, and reputation is like a shadow. The shadow is what we think of it; the tree is the real thing.*
**Abraham Lincoln**

Reading a story about being fit for a Styrofoam cup, hearing how amazing my wife is, and seeing where John Wooden focused his life hopefully inspires you. But how do you discover who you are? How can you figure out your true identity so you are not distracted by all the temptations of this world or lured by false idols?

For me, seeking my identity became vital once I became a father. Before that, I would have had some idea of who I was and what characteristics helped me to do all that I did, but I wouldn't have been able to tell you who I was precisely. When I became a dad, I knew it was time to get focused. If I was going to lead my children and my family, I needed to know who I was and seek to teach my values to my children.

Clearly, defining your values can be challenging. I would encourage you to start with one or more of the many personality tests that exist, like Strengths Finder or Myers Briggs. These unique tools can give insight into your tendencies and personalities. They do not tell you who you are but can help you start to get an idea and begin the process. They are easy to take and are crazy accurate. It usually freaks me out a little because they are so spot-on. I have no idea how it all works, but it does. Visit https://infinitestrengths.com/distracted-by-success/ for a list of personality tests and links to access them.

To establish our family values, my wife and I discussed what we wanted to be known for and who we wanted our children to become. We both agreed that we wanted to become morally sound men and women. We wanted to behave as such and teach our kids to do the same. This meant we first had to define what a morally sound man or woman looked like. To figure this out, we began looking at a list of positive traits, like the one provided by ChatGPT on the next page and highlighted all the values that spoke to us, the ones we felt were vital to living life well. I want you to do this activity. Envision who you want to be, and then go through this list and check all the traits you believe describe your identity.

- Adaptable
- Adventurous
- Affectionate
- Ambitious
- Authentic
- Caring
- Charismatic
- Charming
- Cheerful
- Compassionate
- Confident
- Considerate
- Cooperative
- Courageous
- Creative
- Curious
- Decisive
- Dependable
- Determined
- Diligent
- Empathetic
- Energetic
- Enthusiastic
- Flexible
- Forgiving
- Faithful
- Generous
- Gentle
- Grateful
- Honest
- Humble
- Imaginative

- Independent
- Innovative
- Insightful
- Inspirational
- Intelligent
- Intuitive
- Joyful
- Kind
- Knowledgeable
- Loyal
- Motivated
- Nurturing
- Open-minded
- Optimistic
- Organized
- Passionate
- Patient
- Peaceful
- Perceptive
- Persistent
- Persuasive
- Positive
- Pragmatic
- Proactive
- Reliable
- Resourceful
- Respectful
- Responsible
- Self-assured
- Self-disciplined
- Self-aware
- Sincere

- Supportive
- Sympathetic
- Tactful
- Tenacious
- Thoughtful
- Trustworthy
- Understanding
- Versatile
- Warm-hearted
- Wise
- Witty
- Youthful
- Zealous
- Other

After our first round of looking over the list, my wife and I had many values highlighted. So, we began narrowing them down by discussing which values we felt most strongly about and which we truly wanted to encourage and model in our home. We also asked the people closest to us to share one word they would use to describe us. We wanted to discover what we were indeed known for and how others perceived us. We asked family, friends, colleagues, neighbors, clients, and our pastor. We wanted to check for consistency and see if we were the same people, regardless of where we were or who we were with.

You should do the same. Today, ask at least five people what one word they would use to describe you. Highlighting a list of positive traits is great, but if they are just cool words and aren't you, then they don't matter. Wanting to be known as a trustworthy person and being a trustworthy person are two different things. Find out what others think of you. Ask your team what it's like for you to lead them. Find out what it's like to be married to you or parented by you. Listen to these words and make a separate list.

## WRITE YOUR LIST HERE:

After compiling the list of unique words shared by our community, my wife and I began consolidating our list of positive traits. We eventually narrowed our list to the six values below. These are what we feel characterize a morally sound man or woman.

Being:

- A Person of Faith
- A Person of Integrity
- Courageous
- Responsible
- Persistent
- A Person of Action.

These six characteristics are now our family values. They are the foundation of who we are, who we want to be, how we behave, and what we strive to instill in those around us, most importantly in our children.

Start to consolidate your list.

## WHAT ARE YOUR TOP VALUES?

## WHEN YOU COMPARE THE WORDS PEOPLE USE TO DESCRIBE YOU AND THE WORDS YOU HIGHLIGHTED, WHICH VALUES MATCH?

## WHAT WORDS DID NOT OVERLAP?

## ARE YOU SURPRISED BY ANYTHING?

As you compare your two lists, pick out the words that overlap and best describe you. Choose the traits you know have led to your successes and those that leave you feeling empty, guilty, or regretful when neglected. These behaviors must be, or must become, deeply held values, not necessarily what you value, but traits, characteristics, and behaviors you possess or strive to possess in all situations. I don't care how many values are on your final list, but you must have at least one. You must have one or more characteristics that define you and that you will use to guide your behaviors, thoughts, and actions.

Once you've selected your values, it is time to define them. Because here's the thing: How does one teach, coach, and measure Faith, Integrity, or Courage? Sure, these traits sound great, but what are they? How do you measure if you are living these values or not? Defining each value is critical because we all want to be known as hardworking, loyal, and disciplined. Most of us think we are people of integrity, trustworthiness, and commitment, but sometimes we're not. Many of us are these people and use these values to make decisions, but we don't know how to teach these values to other people. We don't know how to coach them, so we cannot pass down these vital characteristics to the people we care about the most.

To ensure that my wife and I not only lived our values but were also able to teach them to our children, we turned our values into verbs. We made them actions so we could measure our behaviors and then hold our children accountable to the same Standard.

**To Be a Person of Faith:** You must love God with your heart, soul, mind, and body. You do this by treating others the way you want to be treated. You show this by loving yourself, respecting your body, and feeding your mind positive messages. You do this by spending time with God and in his Word.

**To Be a Person of Integrity:** You must do the right things, regardless of who is watching. It is easy to do things the right way, work hard, and be kind when people are watching. But how do you act when you're stuck in traffic? What are you searching for online when no one is watching? How do you behave when you're with your friends or by yourself?

**To Be Courageous,** You must tackle your fears. It's okay and expected to be afraid, but great men and women do not allow these fears to prevent them from moving forward. Instead, they attack their fears with action. They speak up for what is right when no one else will. They try new things, fail, and learn. Courageous people aren't worried about what others think, aren't trying to please everyone, and are okay with upsetting someone, but only when it is necessary.

**To Be Responsible:** You don't give excuses. Regardless of where you're at or what's gone on, you are responsible for what you do and where you're going. You are either creating or allowing everything that happens in your life. When you own this fact, anything is possible, and you will own your life.

**To Be Persistent:** You do not quit. You adapt, pivot, and adjust, but never quit. I don't care how difficult it is or what challenges come your way; a morally sound man or woman won't quit. They will find a way!

**To Be a Person of Action:** You must act when it's time to act. You don't wait on others or find the time; you get things done. You don't confuse emoting about a topic with actually doing something about it - you do it!

Once we defined our values, my wife and I could more easily measure our behaviors. We could tell if we were treating people the right way, doing the right things, not giving excuses, or simply providing lip service. This clarity makes it easier for us to do what we say we will do. This clarity sets the expectation, and then we must follow it. At the same time, turning our values into verbs gives us actions to teach. These values are really all we teach. We know that if our children are people of faith, do the right things, never quit, tackle their fears, take responsibility for their actions, and get things done, nothing else matters. We don't micromanage their grades, reward them for their performance, or chastise them when they don't; we parent the values. Because we know that when they are a morally sound man or woman, they will have good grades, perform well, or will figure it out when they don't. By recognizing their values and not their performance, our kids aren't trying to earn our love. They aren't devastated if they get a B in a class or fear we will berate them on the car ride home after a disappointing game or performance. They know they are loved for who they are, not for their achievements. If they aren't behaving in the right way, that is corrected because they aren't meeting the Standard.

Notice that I said, "The Standard." Our values become our Standard, and they become the way we live, act, and behave regardless of what's going on around us. As Pittsburgh Steeler's football coach Mike Tomlin said, "The

**NO MATTER WHAT HAPPENS, WE KNOW WHO WE ARE AND HOW WE ARE SUPPOSED TO BEHAVE.**

standard is the Standard." If we win, great, go treat people kindly, do the right thing, and get back to work. If we get beaten, bummer, treat people kindly, do the right thing, and get back to work. This Standard simplifies our lives and guides us because no matter what happens, we know who we are and how we are supposed to behave. We could be transitioning from one stage of life to another, our kids could break up with a boyfriend or girlfriend, they could be at a party with their friends, we could be by ourselves, and it doesn't matter. We all know what is expected. When we live by our Standard, we eliminate destructive decisions. We eliminate the guilt that can come from unethical behavior. We are morally sound men and women, and this is what makes us successful.

## WHAT ARE THE FINAL TRAITS THAT WILL MAKE UP YOUR STANDARD?

Now that you have your list of traits written down, your next step is to define them and turn them into actions. These definitions don't have to be cute or creative; they should be short, simple, applicable, and make sense to you. They must also be easy to measure and teach. Take some time defining your traits and write the definitions below.

## DEFINE YOUR TRAITS HERE:
## TRAIT ONE:


## TRAIT TWO:


## TRAIT THREE:


## TRAIT FOUR:


## TRAIT FIVE:


## TRAIT SIX:


These behaviors now become your identity, your Standard, regardless of where you're at or who you're with. These behaviors will dictate how you think, act, and whom you hang out with. They will determine who you date, where you work, the clients you bring on, and every decision you make. Why? Because if or when you violate one of these, you know you are setting yourself up to be miserable, face a ton of guilt, and risk destroying your reputation.

For instance, think of the world of professional sports. If you don't win, then you're out. This pressure encourages some organizations to do whatever winning takes, even if that means violating ethical standards. Recall the 2017 Houston Astros, who resorted to illicit means by employing video cameras to zoom in on the catchers' signals covertly. They subsequently relayed this information to their batters via a concealed buzzer beneath their jerseys. Armed with this unfair advantage, the Houston Astros hitters knew what pitch was coming and successfully crushed the opposing pitchers, which helped them win the Major League Baseball World Series. However, when discovered, their actions came at a high cost, leading to the dismissal of the team's manager and other team leaders, tarnished reputations, and a significant loss of respect for the game. (Vigdor, 2020)

This unethical behavior doesn't only exist in the professional sporting world. Recall the Purdue Pharma opioid scandal. If you Google search Purdue Pharma's code of ethics, you'll find that they pride themselves on being people who do not tolerate human rights abuses within their business operations. They expect all their business partners, including suppliers, to engage in sound human rights practices and treat workers fairly and with dignity and respect. However, Purdue Pharma's most recent Opioid Scandal culminated in their pleading guilty to three felony offenses for deceptively marketing and promoting the highly addictive opioid, OxyContin, to healthcare professionals. The company amassed billions of dollars by aggressively pushing a product they knew to be addictive and was responsible for the deaths of hundreds of thousands of people. Yet this staggering loss of life did not deter their profit-seeking motives. (Deputy Attorney General, 2020)

Claiming to be one thing and living it are two completely different things. Anyone can claim to be a great person; most of us believe that we are great people. What matters are your actions every day?

Knowing and living your Standard is the first fundamental step in living without regret. Once you know who you are, there is no guessing how you should behave. Once you know your identity, you must be yourself, and this can give you the confidence to try new things, see failure as learning, have difficult conversations, choose your friends, and not fall prey to all the distractions of this world. Your Standard humbles you and ensures that you are fit to drink from a Styrofoam cup. Living your values ensures that you are the same moral person, regardless of all the accolades that you receive. This authenticity keeps you from making destructive decisions, which ultimately removes a ton of guilt and regret.

## WHAT'S YOUR STANDARD?

Please share your Standard on our Distracted by Success Facebook Community. It's incredible what can happen to our actions when we tell others who we are and want to be.

www.facebook.com/groups/distractedbysuccess/

ROAD TO SUCCESS
# STAGE TWO: CHANGE YOUR THOUGHTS

# STAGE TWO: CHANGE YOUR THOUGHTS
# CHAPTER 7: DISTRACTED THINKING

*"Misery is almost always the result of thinking."*
— **Joseph Joubert**

Have you ever had a bad day? Have you ever thought that maybe your day had a bad you? Perhaps the day had nothing to do with it. Perhaps you showed up with a bad attitude, weren't prepared, were distracted by the noise, and your day wasn't great because you weren't at your best. How we think about things is typically what makes them so.

**HAVE YOU EVER THOUGHT THAT MAYBE YOUR DAY HAD A BAD YOU?**

If you live for the weekends, what happens to your mood when you realize that tomorrow is Monday? What happens to your thoughts and excitement when you leave work on Fridays? What happens to your mood when you think about an upcoming vacation?

When you were a child, what was your mood like the night before Christmas or summer break? Did it matter how tired or sick you were if you knew Santa was coming that night or if school was done for the summer? Your answer is, most likely, no. Why? Because of how you thought. The sun rose and set the same on those days as every other day. It's how you thought about those days which impacted everything. What the day meant or what you had planned for that day determined if you were excited about it or dreading it.

Regardless of how you think, you are right. If you feel your boss dislikes you, you will find examples that reinforce that belief. If you believe your team is lazy, you will find examples of them being lazy. If you think you're not worthy, unattractive, or destined for failure, guess what? You will find examples that back up those beliefs. If you think you're great, beautiful, and can do whatever you want, then you can. Why? Because of the messages you are telling yourself and the attitude that stems from those messages.

According to author and former mental skills coach Trevor Moawad, "Negative thoughts are four to seven times more powerful than positivity, and these same thoughts become ten times more powerful when you actually say them out loud" (Moawad, 20). We talk to ourselves more than we talk to anyone else. We constantly give ourselves messages throughout the day that either build us up or destroy our psyche. Are you your biggest fan or worst critic?

Trevor Moawad's insight is so powerful because the National Science Foundation found that we have, on average, 60,000 thoughts a day; of those thoughts, 80 percent are negative. We are telling ourselves that we can't do something, that we aren't good enough, that we are ugly, not fast enough, weak, and just plain stink. What's even crazier is that the study highlights that 57,000 of these thoughts are the same ones we had yesterday. (National Science Foundation, 2012) That's right, 57,000 thoughts are the same old tune replaying in our brains daily. They become the narrative of our lives. What happens if our story has us playing the victim instead of the victor?

Many of us get so caught up in the past that it prevents us from moving forward. We believe that because we failed before, messed up a relationship, were born in the projects, were raised in an abusive home, are dyslexic, or have some ailment, that somehow, these hardships make us destined for disaster. Many of us convince ourselves that our past controls our future. Thus, we live an endless life of despair, never able to escape the grip of our own thoughts.

Others don't live in the negative past, but instead, they live back in the good ole glory days. They believe they have already done the most significant things they will ever do. Maybe you were valedictorian, and don't think you'll ever be able to top that. Perhaps you won a championship in high school, college, or the pros and believe that is your life's pinnacle. Maybe you had your dream job, a great relationship, raised a beautiful family, and have thought those are the most significant things you will ever do. This type of thinking allows depression to set in. You might not see the point of getting up, going on, or trying anything new because you think your greatest accomplishments are behind you. Living in the past only leads to depression, regardless of whether the thoughts are negative or positive. It prevents you from moving forward and onward to a new adventure or life mission. Consistently thinking of the past is a distraction that keeps you from a successful future.

At the same time, living in the future doesn't serve us well either. Continually thinking about what is to come can lead to anxiety. Unfortunately, many of us are so concerned about the future that we become too paranoid to move. This anxiety and worry leads to fear, which can be paralyzing.

How many people do you know who have stayed in an abusive relationship because they fear being alone? People would rather stay with the devil they know than be with the angel they have never met. How many people stay in an awful job because they fear no one else will hire them? They stick to a monotonous routine or deal with the same abusive boss because they have become comfortable or because they have good benefits. They know a paycheck is coming. They are willing to be unhappy where they are, fearing the unknown future could be worse.

**BEGIN TO REGRET THE DREAMS WE DIDN'T PURSUE.**

How many people don't pursue their dreams because of fear? They fear failure, rejection, and what others might think. This fear distracts them and encourages them to seek safety instead of fulfilling their greatness. People stick to what they know because the risk of failing and being thought a fool is too high.

Some don't go after their dreams because they fear success. They fear they might actually be good at it, and then what? They would have to do more of it and continue to perform, which can cause too much pressure. As we age, we are more and more likely to regret the things we didn't try; we begin to regret the dreams we didn't pursue.

Irrational Fears are not real; though they are powerful, they are entirely made up. This means that to overcome them, we merely need to create and execute a better plan. You need to attack your fears with action, which will change your thinking. Too many of us associate fear with danger; they are not the same. Dangers are real and must be avoided. A rattlesnake is dangerous, playing with a loaded gun is dangerous, and doing drugs is dangerous. Don't mess with these things. But the fear of what others think of you, public speaking, heights, or a fear of what the future might bring, though powerful, are nothing more than figments of our imagination. They are not dangerous. They are make-believe, which means you can rewrite the script and break through your fears.

> **FEARS ARE NOT REAL; THOUGH THEY ARE POWERFUL, THEY ARE ENTIRELY MADE UP.**

With no risk, there is no reward. To achieve your dreams, you must be willing to take risks. To meet your spouse, you had to take a risk. You had to initiate the conversation, go on a first date, and take a chance at being rejected. To get a job, you must take a chance and go to an interview or apply for a promotion. We must risk a lot to start our own business, move to a new state, change careers, or get out of an unhealthy relationship. Having children includes risks of financial strain, loss of freedom, and could impact your career.

To love might require the most risk of all, as there is a chance of a broken heart. Throughout your life, there will certainly be loss, struggle, challenges, and even death. They are guaranteed. But without love, you really have nothing. We deny ourselves happiness if we

> **WITHOUT LOVE, YOU REALLY HAVE NOTHING.**

have no one to love. Even with all the sorrow and heartbreak that can come with love, it is always worth the risk.

There is a significant difference between being risky and being reckless. Many people confuse the two, become distracted, and ultimately fail. Being risky is being presented with an opportunity, playing out the worst-case scenario, and deciding if you can live with that outcome. If you can, then roll the dice; it is worth the risk. It's not that you want the worst thing to happen; it's just that you know you'll be okay if it does. On the other hand, Reckless is being presented with an opportunity where you cannot live with the worst-case scenario yet decide to move forward anyway. This is reckless because if the worst case happens, you may not recover. You should avoid being reckless. Know that what is considered reckless changes based on your age, responsibilities, and wisdom.

For example, moving away for college. This is a significant decision and can be extremely scary. But what's the worst thing that could happen? You don't like it and come home after your first year. This seems like a minimal price to pay for the amount of personal growth, new friends, experiences, and wisdom you could gain. What's the worst thing that could happen if you start your own business? Perhaps it doesn't work, and you must get a job working elsewhere. Once again, that seems like an exceedingly small price to pay for the opportunity to achieve your dreams and do what you've always wanted. Unfortunately, too many of us don't pre-plan this way. We don't play out the actual worst-case scenario; instead, we fabricate illusions of destruction, which causes fear and prevents us from moving forward.

Others tend to imagine all the greener grass on the other side and only envision the wins, titles, and enjoyment. Then, they begin the journey and discover that it is much more complex than they imagined. They realize that the greener grass isn't all that green after all, and this lack of fulfillment causes regret and encourages them to quit and never try again.

Only playing out the worst-case scenario can be just as harmful as only playing out the best-case scenario. Each is a possibility, and you must think them through before beginning. If you don't think through all logical outcomes, you are likely to be surprised when your journey begins and the unexpected challenges bring your mission to a screeching halt. When you accurately acknowledge the worst possible outcomes and start anyway, you are less likely to be surprised. You won't be disappointed and will have a much more accurate picture of the work required to achieve your dreams.

Being able to live a life without regret isn't about having no fears, no worries, or no stress. It's about leaning into these difficulties and looking at them objectively. It's acknowledging these adversities and finding a way to move beyond them or use them to grow you instead of holding you back.

Fear can be good if we use it to improve us. Fear is a powerful emotion that can get us to move and take action. For instance, I get a little nervous when I speak in front of large crowds, but the fear doesn't prevent me from doing it. It causes me to become exceptionally prepared. My fear pushes me to work hard and ensure I really know my material. I don't walk on the stage wondering if I prepared enough, wondering if I'm ready. I know I am and that I've got my stuff down. I know I've done the work because my fears drive me to action. By the time I walk on stage, I have practiced my speech so many times I can do it in my sleep.

**FEAR CAN BE GOOD IF WE USE IT TO IMPROVE US.**

I also fear not being perceived as credible or being taken seriously by others, and I worry about wasting people's time. However, these don't prevent me from leading teams or making decisions because I use this fear to push me. Not wanting to appear dumb or incompetent challenges me to learn as much as possible. I ask many more questions than the number of answers I give. Fearing that I could be wasting people's time ensures that I am organized, have a plan, and then execute that plan. I will never meet just to meet. I don't start meetings late or run them over the allotted time because I don't want to distract people, make them feel like I don't respect their time, or come across as unorganized. Once again, my fears don't prevent me from moving; they drive me to improve and be my best.

## WHAT ARE YOUR FEARS?

# HOW CAN YOU USE YOUR FEAR TO HELP YOU IMPROVE AND BE YOUR BEST?

When you distract your thoughts with worry, you are praying for bad things to happen. When you live in the past, you are prevented from maximizing the now. When you have a bad day, it is usually because you were not at your best. But as you will learn, successful people don't have bad days. Sure, they will

## SUCCESSFUL PEOPLE THINK DIFFERENTLY.

have bad moments, but they don't have bad days, and a lot of this has to do with how they think. You will learn that successful people think differently. They aren't naively positive, nor do they think that everything is doom and gloom. Instead, they are optimistic and hopeful; regardless of what life throws at them, they know they control how they think. It's this way of thinking that gives them freedom. Their thinking propels them forward and prevents them from having regrets.

Before we jump into how the greats think, reflect on the below circumstances.

# HOW DO YOU RESPOND TO THE NEGATIVE THINGS IN YOUR LIFE?

# HOW DO YOU REACT WHEN THINGS DON'T GO AS PLANNED?

# HOW DO YOU BEHAVE WHEN SOMEONE CUTS YOU OFF ON THE FREEWAY OR YOU HAVE TO DEAL WITH SOMEONE WHO APPEARS INCOMPETENT?

DO YOUR RESPONSES MAKE SITUATIONS BETTER OR WORSE?


ARE YOU FIXATED ON THE NEGATIVE IN FRUSTRATING SITUATIONS OR FOCUSED ON FINDING A SOLUTION?

# STAGE TWO: CHANGE YOUR THOUGHTS
# CHAPTER 8: THE GREATS THOUGHTS

*Most people don't grow up. It's too difficult. What happens is most people get older.*
**Maya Angelou**

When you sit back and look at the greats, you'll find that every one of them has issues, just like you and me. They have deadlines. They have employees who fail to do what they say. They get stressed. They get sick, must deal with death, have been turned down for opportunities, and even have financial concerns. They have children who are crazy, deal with aging, get stuck in traffic, have plumbing problems, and on and on and on. Yet the greats never sulk over these issues. They don't allow such things to prevent them from moving forward or pretend that these events have any bearing on the rest of their day.

The greats, as Duke University Women's Basketball Coach Kara Lawson said, "have learned to handle difficult things better." Their life isn't easy; they don't coast or take the lazy route. The greats have just done hard things and learned to handle all the challenges. You can see her talk by visiting our Distracted by Success webpage https://infinitestrengths.com/distracted-by-success/

Successful people know they have no idea what might happen on any given day. An infinite number of things could positively or negatively affect their personal lives, professional lives, or relationships over which they have zero control. There could be a car wreck, someone could get diagnosed with cancer, the government could shut down, or interest rates could spike. There could be a fire, natural disaster, a war, or an economic recession. It's not that these things don't impact the greats. They do. However, successful people don't allow these challenges to prevent them from moving forward. They don't fall prey to their circumstances. It doesn't mean they are happy about the challenges or thrilled about all the obstacles they face. It is just that they refuse to stay negative about them. They are, as Trevor Moawad would say, "Neutral with their thinking." (Moawad, 2020) They aren't negative or positive. They are just neutral, accepting that something happened, learning from it, and then figuring out how to move forward. They don't pretend that everything is just glorious when it's not. Not everything in life is great. Striking out to lose a game, bombing a presentation, losing a big client, or finding out that your spouse is leaving you aren't positive. Yet, if you stay negative after these events, you prevent yourself from moving forward. Inversely, if you pretend that everything is peachy, you often fail to see the severity of the situation and can't learn from it.

Successful people choose to think differently. Sure, life is hard, but compared to what? Life just is! It's how you think about your life that makes it so. Now, I'm not saying that there aren't more difficult lives than others, and life sure as heck isn't easy for everyone. But when you start comparing your life to others, you do yourself an injustice. You start creating excuses and can fail to rise from your challenges. Emerging from what life throws at you, gaining a new perspective after a tough loss, or learning a new skill after facing many of life's unforeseen obstacles doesn't mean that everything happens for a reason. I don't believe that. I believe

**REGARDLESS OF WHAT THE GREATS GO THROUGH, THEY GAIN NEW PERSPECTIVES, LEARN NEW SKILLS, ACQUIRE NEW TECHNIQUES, BUILD BETTER RELATIONSHIPS, AND FIND A WAY TO GROW THROUGH THE ADVERSITY THEY ARE IMMERSED IN.**

that you find a reason when you think neutrally, keep moving forward, learn from your experiences, and do not allow yourself to play the victim. When you grow and create positive outcomes from the pain you have gone through, it doesn't make everything worth it; it's just that your growth keeps you from wasting your pain. Regardless of what the greats go through, they gain new perspectives, learn new skills, acquire new techniques, build better relationships, and find a way to grow through the adversity they are immersed in.

Unfortunately, too many people waste their pain. We go through challenges and face obstacles, and instead of learning from them, we continue to make the same mistakes. How many people have you seen go from one troubled relationship to another and are stuck in an endless cycle of abuse and distrust? How many companies consistently hire the wrong type of person or bring on the wrong kinds of clients? Their failure to change and learn from mistakes ends up killing the organization. How many people put on a lot of weight, lose a lot of weight, and then put on even more? How many people were raised in an abusive household and then grew up to become abusive themselves? How many of us have lost loved ones yet still haven't realized that life isn't about money, gaining power, winning, or fame?

Successful people never waste their pain. They acknowledge the reality of the situation, stay neutral, and then get into action. Sure, they get upset and negative, but they don't stay there. They keep moving and gain new perspectives or learn new strategies. It's important to note that emerging through a crisis and gaining something from our pain doesn't mean that the knowledge or wisdom acquired from that experience was worth all the pain and suffering you went through. It doesn't mean that the greats are happy it happened. It doesn't mean they enjoyed the process or believed that the outcome or opportunity was equal to or greater than the fight. They merely emerged and learned something that made them stronger, gave them wisdom, or developed a new trait that could be helpful in the future. For instance, we have all lost a loved one, and for many of us, this loss puts life in perspective. It teaches us to spend time and be more present

**SUCCESSFUL PEOPLE NEVER WASTE THEIR PAIN.**

with those we love, cherish life, and go after our dreams. Though these lessons are significant, we would much rather have learned them and still had our loved ones with us. Gaining these perspectives doesn't mean that the death of our loved one was worth it. It's just that we aren't going to go through a challenging event, not gain something, and then repeat the same selfish mistakes. The greats have gone through hard things and have learned to handle them better. This type of thinking separates the most successful people from everyone else. To best see how the greats think, I want to share a short story on the life of Frederick Douglass.

Frederick Douglass was born into slavery in Maryland around 1817. As a child, he was separated from his mother and given to a caretaker who later died. Frederick was then sold to an owner on the coast of Maryland. At the time, it was illegal to teach an enslaved person to read. However, the wife of his master began teaching Frederick the alphabet. The little she managed to teach him before her husband discovered it altered Frederick's belief in what was possible. From that point forward, regardless of what society and the world said about him, he believed he was something more significant than an enslaved person. Frederick desperately wanted to learn to read and write, so he pursued every opportunity for education. He would sneak into his master's children's room, open their schoolbooks, and begin tracing the letters to learn how to write. He would go down to the shipyard and offer white schoolboys bread if they could read the words on newspapers or the sides of ships. Frederick would memorize the words, eventually teaching himself to read and write. When it was discovered that Frederick was educated, he was sold to an inland plantation. He had to spend time with one of the fiercest slave trainers, whose job was to beat enslaved people until they were broken mentally and would follow their master's orders. Even amidst these horrible circumstances, Frederick Douglass had the belief that he was more than an enslaved person. He knew this was no life for him. Eventually, Douglass had enough and attacked the slave trainer, beating him to an inch of his life. Expecting death, Frederick was amazed that this fierce trainer was afraid of losing his business, so he gave no consequence.

A short time later, Douglass escaped and headed north, where a religious organization eventually bought him his freedom. Douglass could now fulfill his inner self-belief and become more than an enslaved person. Now freed, Frederick Douglass became one of the best orators of his generation, publishing a newspaper and fighting for Civil Rights. Partly because of Douglass's contributions, President Lincoln authorized the first All-Black 54th Massachusetts Regiment that fought in the Civil War, and later, Lincoln signed the Emancipation Proclamation in 1863, making slavery illegal in the States of Rebellion. Following the Civil War, Frederick Douglass went on to fight for Women's Suffrage and even garnered votes for the President of the United States in 1872. (Douglass, 1845)

This is one of my favorite stories because it highlights what can happen when we don't let our circumstances define us. Frederick Douglass could have given every excuse in the book, and every one of them would have been justified. This man was flat-out a victim, yet he didn't fall into victimhood. He wasn't positive or happy about his situation, but he wouldn't allow it to prevent him from becoming who he knew he was. What he gained and acquired wasn't worth all the anguish, pain, and sorrow he experienced. However, he didn't waste the pain either. He was either going to be killed or succeed.

**CHOOSING TO BE OPTIMISTIC DOESN'T MAKE LIFE EASIER; IT JUST GIVES YOU MORE POSSIBILITIES.**

Thankfully, very few of us have gone through something as horrific as Frederick's childhood, yet so many of us are allowing our challenges, hardships, and struggles to prevent us from moving forward. Choosing to be optimistic doesn't make life easier; it just gives you more possibilities. We can't prevent challenging things from happening to us, but we can choose how we let those things affect our thoughts. When we learn to do this, there will be nothing that can keep us from achieving success.

Remember that success doesn't mean you'll get everything you want. It means you'll have the freedom to do whatever needs to be done and keep moving forward because what you believe is possible has expanded.

The ability to control your thoughts amidst chaos makes the men and women serving in our military so special. I don't admire them for their rank, the size of their biceps, or how much influence they have. I admire them for their sacrifice, bravery, and ability to do what hardly any of us are willing to do. When things are at their worst, you will find the men and women of our military at their best. A reason for this is because of how they think. For instance, my great friend and mentor, Gary Denham, a retired Navy SEAL, spoke about this ability to think. He said, "that we overtrain to automaticity. This allows us to fall back on training, especially in the heat of the battle. This overtraining frees our conscious mind to focus on the task, not being distracted by the fog of war." The Navy SEALs can think while their enemy is frozen. They can stay calm and make the right moves while everyone else is in chaos. This thinking doesn't happen by chance. It isn't just reserved for some and not for others. They have trained hard and continue to train harder, allowing them to handle hard better. This means that you can do the same. It means you can learn to think differently to live a life of no regrets.

## HOW DO YOU THINK?

## DO YOU STAY NEUTRAL AND KEEP GOING, OR DO YOU SULK OVER THE NEGATIVE, WHICH PREVENTS YOU FROM MOVING FORWARD?

## WHAT OBSTACLES HAVE YOU CLAIMED HOLD YOU BACK?
## HOW CAN YOU USE THOSE OBSTACLES TO MAKE YOU BETTER?

## STAGE TWO: CHANGE YOUR THOUGHTS
# CHAPTER 9: HOW TO THINK DIFFERENTLY

*"Be Curious, Not Judgmental"*
**Walt Whitman**

So, how do you change your thinking and learn to think differently? How do you lea rn to keep moving when times get hard? How do you learn to stay calm or neutral when times get challenging? How do you ensure you keep growing and getting better?

First, you must know who you are. Confidence stems from your identity, and when your identity is wrapped around your values, you know exactly who you are and how you are supposed to behave in every circumstance. When you live by your values, you're assured your behaviors are in check; you won't make destructive decisions. That's your Standard. Regardless of what's happening around you, you know your response will be as a person of integrity who is responsible, courageous, persistent, takes action, and treats people how they want to be treated. You can always be this person. You can.

Second, you must grow your wisdom. Wisdom is key because it gives you the knowledge and awareness to best interact with the world. Wisdom gives you the superpower to handle whatever the world throws at you. Wisdom is what determines if you are growing up or merely getting older. When you acquire wisdom, your thinking changes, your actions change, and your perspective changes. In other words, you grow up. Without it, you get stuck in your ways, dwell on the past, or fear the future. All these factors prevent you from living a successful life.

Acquiring wisdom improves your thinking, but you must first know what wisdom means in order to seek it.

I believe wisdom is comprised of 3 things.

1. **Knowledge:** You can't be wise if you are clueless. Think about how foolish you feel when you are in a situation where you haven't yet developed the knowledge to be effective. I was ignorant when I came home from the hospital with our first child. I wasn't confident, I was fearful, and I couldn't believe that the hospital let my wife and I leave with a baby. By the time we had a third child, that fear was gone. Why? Because we had done it before. We had already learned how to take care of a baby. Think of how clueless you feel when you take on a new job. You feel inadequate because you don't have the knowledge to perform in your new role effectively. But after time, you gain experience, skills, and confidence.

   Knowledge is a combination of book smarts and your IQ, and you should never stop acquiring more knowledge. Once you do, you stop being wise. Your thinking becomes archaic, and the information that you share can become irrelevant. Imagine you work in the tech field and decide that you no longer need to acquire any more knowledge. You believe that you know enough. How long before you become irrelevant?

   To gain wisdom, you must constantly learn new things, new ways, and gain as much knowledge as possible, or your thinking will become stale.

2. **Awareness:**    How unwise does someone look when they are unaware of their surroundings? How silly does the athlete look when they are unaware of what is happening around them on the field or the court? How foolish does that genius appear when they are unaware of how to communicate their ideas? How ridiculous does the boss look when she believes she is challenging her people yet is unaware that her tactics come across as abrasive and condescending?

Awareness, to me, is our street smarts; it's our emotional intelligence. If you lack this, you will struggle to build relationships, communicate, and know what's really going on around you. You will be unable to empathize with the world. Having zero to little awareness prevents you from being able to think productively and neutrally. You won't be able to make the best decisions because you cannot grasp the severity of the situation. Thus, you could panic or not respond quickly enough because of your lack of awareness.

3. **Action:** How unwise do you look when you know precisely what to do but don't do it? You look silly when you know you should exercise and eat healthy to live a long and fruitful life, yet you don't do it. You are unwise when you know that the people in your family are the most important things in your life, yet you don't make any time to show them. You are foolish when your mantra is, "Do as I say, not as I do?"

If you want to improve your thinking, you must act. Even if you acquire all the knowledge in the world and have the highest EQ score ever, you are not wise if you don't put this knowledge and empathy into practice.

So, if wisdom is knowledge, awareness, and increased accountability to do what we know we should, how do we acquire it? Where can we find wisdom so we can constantly improve our thinking?

I seek it in three ways and challenge you to do the same.

# ACQUIRING WISDOM
## STEP ONE: SEEK MENTORSHIP

### WHO ARE YOUR MENTORS?

### HOW OFTEN DO YOU MEET WITH YOUR MENTORS?

### WHEN YOU SPEAK WITH THEM, HOW DO YOU FEEL?

### WHAT DO YOU LEARN FROM YOUR MENTORS?

I would bet that you feel encouraged, learn new things, gain new perspectives, and are more committed because you don't want to let your mentor down. By speaking with your mentor, you gain more knowledge, increase your awareness, and are more likely to do what you said you were going to do, all of which increase your wisdom.

If that's the case, shouldn't you have more mentors? And shouldn't you be speaking with them more often?

If you gain more wisdom every time you speak to a mentor, why wouldn't you want to find as many as you can and connect with them as often as you can?

Unfortunately, I have found that most people have, on average, 2-3 mentors and only speak with them occasionally. This is better than zero, but what happens if one of them passes away? What happens if you overextend your welcome?

What happens if your 2-3 mentors think, act, and believe the same things? What happens if you're not gaining different perspectives from different demographics? You don't have to agree with everything you hear, but hearing it is essential to grow and continue growing.

When you look at the most successful people in the world, they have a plethora of mentors from all walks of life. Their mentors are old and young, male and female, of different ethnicities, part of various political parties, and involved in other industries. Why? Because diversity provides diverse wisdom. It gives a wide range of new information, provides varying perspectives, and gives the wisdom required to think differently. If you want to understand the youth better, you need to connect with people younger than you. If you want to know about the struggles that persist within a minority community, then you need to seek mentorship from someone within that community. Without this, you are missing essential pieces of the whole picture, and your education and wisdom will be lacking.

If you want to improve your thinking, surround yourself with people who think differently. Again, this doesn't mean that you must agree with them; it doesn't mean that that person must be a mentor in every aspect of your life. I have several people who are amazing mentors within their fields, but they are trainwrecks in others. I do not seek guidance from them in those areas. For instance, when I was in college, my strength coach was one of the best in the industry. He knew more about fitness than all my other strength coaches combined, but he was a mess when it came to relationships. So, he was my mentor regarding strength training, but I would have never sought his advice on dating.

Surrounding yourself with fascinating people makes life simpler and more colorful. We gain the resources required to help us think and improve our lives. Have you ever heard the quote by Jim Rohn that says, "We become the average of our five closest friends?" Think about that for a moment. You will be the average of whom you surround yourself with. This means physically, financially, relationally, and spiritually.

**SURROUNDING YOURSELF WITH FASCINATING PEOPLE MAKES LIFE SIMPLER AND MORE COLORFUL.**

When you hang around a bunch of fit people, what happens to your thinking and, eventually, your actions?

When you are around a group of naysayers or cynics, what begins to happen to your attitude and thinking?

What happens to you when you surround yourself with fascinating people who think and act outside the box?

When I was coaching high school baseball in Arizona, we started an alumni home run derby. We brought back many former players who had

## CHANGE YOUR ROOM!

gone on to do amazing things, some of whom played college or professional baseball. In the home run derby, the alumni would compete against our current juniors and seniors, and the entire program would interact with the champions from the past. Amazing things began to happen by surrounding my current players with fascinating, more accomplished players. My players started to visualize themselves as big leaguers; they realized the program they were a part of was something special, something to be proud of, and their thinking changed. My players thought, if this guy can do it, then so can I. Their mindset shift produced 22 MLB draft picks, four big leaguers, over 60 collegiate baseball players, 11 All-Americans, a state championship, and multiple national rankings in 11 years. I share this because the school I coached at was always good, always talented, and always coached by amazing people. They just hadn't yet opened their minds to what was possible. I believe the mind shift was the difference. We showed them a different room. We had our players compete against and sometimes beat current collegiate or professional baseball players, and this changed what our players thought was possible. We elevated the average, and then everything else took care of itself.

If you want to begin changing the way you think and ensure that you live a life without regret, then change your room! Get around people doing and living the life you want, and then get ready for the ride.

# ACQUIRING WISDOM
## STEP TWO: BE INTENTIONAL WITH WHAT YOU FEED YOUR BRAIN

What do you read, listen to, or watch? What types of information do you consume daily? Is it positive or negative? Is it motivational or depressing? Is it teaching you anything or merely filling your mind with useless content?

Yes, Jim Rohn is right, but I believe Charlie Tremendous Jones was even more accurate when he said, "The people you meet and the books you read will impact your next five years more than anything else you do."

Have you ever read a quote, consumed a passage from the Bible, or read a book, and the information changed your way of life? In my third year of coaching, I read the book Season of Life by Jeffery Marx, and this book changed my life. It highlights that we should coach to help children become morally sound men and women. This philosophy changed my entire mission. Why? Because I fed my brain with something that made me see a new and better way and ultimately made me think, live, and coach differently.

Unfortunately, so many of us are not intentional about what we consume. We ignore what goes on in our brains and somehow believe we can magically improve our thoughts and knowledge. If you watch the same news channel daily, what do you think will happen to your thoughts? What happens to your thinking when you only read the same things that your Twitter, Facebook, and TikTok algorithms feed you? Eventually, you stop thinking. Eventually, you become set in your ways and are convinced that anyone who thinks differently than you is wrong.

The greats are very cognizant of what their brains consume. They are constantly feeding their brains information from diverse sources. They seek to gain new perspectives. It is important to learn from opposing sides on topics. If you listen to a podcast on pro-choice, then you should also listen to one on pro-life. If you read a book by President Obama, then you should read one by President Bush. Read blogs written by women and some by men. Watch documentaries highlighting the experiences of African Americans in the South during the 1960s or the life of immigrants within the United States now. This way, you are gaining more wisdom. You are being exposed to new knowledge and different perspectives. You are learning to think differently.

Sometimes, we aren't surrounded by great people. Sometimes, my mentors aren't available, yet I need a new perspective now! I need wisdom, knowledge, and accountability right now. We must know where to turn and what to consume at these moments. If I'm struggling, all I need to do is read a passage in the Bible or listen to a pep talk by Dabo Swinney, the head football coach for Clemson University, and my thoughts change. If I'm tired and don't feel like working out, I can throw on the Rocky Soundtrack, and I'm ready to go. My house starts dancing when I play the song, Timber, by Pit Bull. Why? Because we are feeding our brains with something that excites us and gets our motors revving instead of just staying plopped on the couch.

## WHAT ARE YOU FEEDING YOUR BRAIN ON A CONSISTENT BASIS?

## WHAT BOOKS ARE YOU READING?

Are they helping you acquire more knowledge or gain new perspectives? Or do they only reaffirm your current beliefs?

## WHAT SHOWS OR MOVIES ARE YOU CONSUMING?

Are they challenging your thinking, making you better, and filling you with hope and encouragement, or are they full of dishonesty, cheating, crime, and other distasteful content? No judgment here—just something to reflect on.

## WHAT PEOPLE DO YOU FOLLOW ON SOCIAL MEDIA?
Do they elevate your thoughts or hold you back?


## HOW WILL YOU IMPROVE WHAT YOU ARE FEEDING YOUR BRAIN? WHAT WILL YOU CONSUME? WHEN WILL YOU START? WHERE WILL YOU BE?


# ACQUIRING WISDOM
## STEP THREE: EXPERIENCE NEW THINGS

How do you know unless you know? How foolish do we look if we have an opinion on something we've never experienced? For example, I never understood why anyone would want to eat an oyster. I thought, why would anyone want to consume something resembling snot on a shell? Then, at happy hour one Friday, a friend offered me some of his oyster appetizer. I shared my opinion with him and sounded quite foolish when he asked me if I had ever had one. So, I gave in and finally tried one, and I realized it's awful and tastes like snot on a shell. But at least I now have the experience to back up my opinion.

How can you have an opinion on anything unless you've experienced the situation or at least connected with people who have lived it? Unfortunately, many people make up their minds on a topic once they've read it in a book, seen it online, or just heard someone else talk about it. They don't even fact-check or ensure it is from a reputable source. They take the new information as fact, and it becomes their truth. How do you know that the information you have gathered is correct or if the perspectives are accurate unless you've experienced it yourself or at least ensured your source is reputable?

The greats are constantly experiencing new things. They challenge their thoughts with innovative ideas, seek change, and try to find more efficient ways of doing things. They travel the world, and this opens their minds to new perspectives. They see how others live, experience what is possible, find areas they can improve, and become wiser in the process. When you do this, your perspective changes. The world doesn't change; you change how you see it.

How do you know what's happening inside someone's brain unless you get to know them? How do you know something won't work unless you or your team have tried it? Get outside your comfort zone, meet new people, try new things, and welcome failure and pushback. Growth is worth it.

If you want to learn how to change your thinking, you must experience new things. You must act! Navy SEALS aren't born *organized, trained, and equipped for the most high-level special operations*. They are able to operate on automaticity because of the extreme training they go through. They experience difficult drill after difficult drill, and these new experiences retrain their brains so they can focus on the task instead of the fog of war. They didn't just read about their training or have someone teach them; they did it! The SEALS are willing to experience new and extremely high levels of training so they can become the world's most elite, nimble military warriors.

Richard Branson came up with the idea of Virgin Airways because of an awful experience traveling. His flight from Puerto Rico to the British Virgin Islands had been canceled because the airline said there wasn't enough interest. Desperately wanting to see his wife and believing enough people wanted to fly, Branson rented a plane that day, made a sign, and walked around the airport selling seats for $39 to anyone wanting to get to the British Virgin Islands. He ended up filling the plane, and Virgin Airways was born. (Kupietzky, 2023)

This idea didn't come to him in his sleep or from a fortune teller. He had a bad experience, figured others were having the same, and came up with a solution. His experience gave him the awareness of a need, and he took on the responsibility of making a difference.

## WHEN WAS THE LAST TIME YOU EXPERIENCED SOMETHING NEW THAT VALIDATED ONE OF YOUR BELIEFS?

## WHEN WAS THE LAST TIME YOU EXPERIENCED SOMETHING NEW THAT CHANGED YOUR PERSPECTIVE?

## WHAT ACTIVITIES CAN YOU EXPERIENCE THAT WILL CHALLENGE YOUR THINKING?

## WHERE CAN YOU ADD MORE COMPLEXITY TO YOUR LIFE EXPERIENCES AND TO THE CONTENT YOU FEED TO YOUR BRAIN?

As we age, the number of experiences we are afforded tends to decrease. This could be due to several factors.

## WHAT ARE SOME EXPERIENCES THAT YOU DESPERATELY WANT TO HAVE DURING YOUR LIFE?

## SET A DATE RIGHT NOW FOR WHEN YOU WILL EXPERIENCE THEM. MAKE A PLAN AND MAKE IT HAPPEN.

Successful people aren't successful by luck or chance, and they don't have some exceptional talent that is only reserved for the few. They have learned how to think differently and are never done. They will always seek wisdom, knowing that their thinking will become stale once the pursuit of knowledge ends. And that is when regrets begin to build.

Please share any tips or tricks that you implement to learn to think differently. How do you stay sharp and mentally tough, seek wisdom, and prepare to handle all that life throws at you? Visit our Distracted by Success Facebook Community and learn how others seek Wisdom.

www.facebook.com/groups/distractedbysuccess/

ROAD TO SUCCESS STAGE THREE:
# TAKE ACTION

# STAGE THREE: TAKE ACTION
## CHAPTER 10: DISTRACTED MOTION

*"The most invisible form of wasted time is doing a good job on an unimportant task."*
**James Clear**

Having a Standard, knowing who you want to be, and being able to control your thoughts mean nothing unless you put all of this into action. Saying you are a person of integrity means nothing until you always do the right thing, regardless of who's watching. Believing you are a team player means nothing until you are genuinely excited about the achievement of those around you and bust your tail within your role. Saying you want to be successful means nothing until your actions are successful.

> **SAYING YOU WANT TO BE SUCCESSFUL MEANS NOTHING UNTIL YOUR ACTIONS ARE SUCCESSFUL.**

Interestingly, almost everyone knows what action is required to succeed, but we don't take it.

# IF YOU WANT TO BE HEALTHY, WHAT SHOULD YOU DO?

# WHAT SHOULD YOU DO IF YOU WANT TO HAVE MONEY AVAILABLE FOR RETIREMENT?

# WHAT MUST BE DONE TO IMPROVE YOUR RELATIONSHIPS?

# HOW CAN YOU PERFORM BETTER AT WORK?

# ARE YOU DOING ALL OR ANY OF THOSE THINGS?

Though I am not checking what you wrote, I'm pretty confident that you know the answers to those questions, and I would be willing to bet that you are not executing all of them.

We all know that to be healthy, we should eat better, drink less alcohol, and exercise more, yet according to a national survey completed by USAfacts.org, 70% of American Adults are either overweight or obese. (USAFacts, 23)

We all know that we should save and invest our money so it can work for us. However, according to the Survey of Consumer Finances (SCF), in 2022, almost half of American households had no savings in retirement accounts. Of those that did, only Twenty-six percent had saved more than $100,000. (USAfacts, 23)

We all know that we should treat our spouses with respect, spend time with them, and do the things that make them happy, yet according to the U.S. Census Bureau's statistics on divorce, the U.S. has over 900,000 new divorces each year. (Harper, 24)_

Many coaches have read about John Wooden and know his pyramid of success and how he went about his business. But not many coaches put his principles into practice. Many that I've worked with or seen do not. They know what should be done and might even think they are putting the pyramid of success into action, but they aren't. So many coaches are all talk and no action.

Why do so many of us fail? Because we confuse knowledge with action. We think if we can talk about being great, envision an awesome marriage, read about investments, and talk about being healthy, then it will eventually happen. We tell ourselves we'll start tomorrow or next year, but the time for our consistent action never comes. Knowledge means nothing if we don't back it up with action. We can't talk or think our way out of something that we've acted our way into. We must act our way out of it.

**WE CAN'T TALK OR THINK OUR WAY OUT OF SOMETHING THAT WE'VE ACTED OUR WAY INTO.**

Lack of action is typically met with an excuse, and the excuse becomes the distraction. We argue that we are tired, don't have enough time, claim that it's not our responsibility, are too busy, or don't feel like it. With each excuse, we become a little more distracted, a little more complacent, or as my friend and motivational speaker, "Shep," says, "you become a little more of a loser." Every time you cast blame and fail to take ownership of your life, you become a little more helpless, you become a little more stuck, and you continue to pile up a few more regrets.

It's wild that so many of us have convinced ourselves that we don't have enough time. Yet, I know of single parents raising multiple kids, taking them to all their sporting events, working two jobs, and getting a college degree or a Ph.D. I see CEOs, VPs, coaches, teachers, and doctors who have tremendous families, crushing their careers and impacting lives. At the same time, they are healthy, financially stable, and spiritually sound. Elon Musk has found a way to run five multibillion-dollar companies in the same 24 hours you and I have. These people don't have more time than us; they aren't given some secret code to get the most out of life. They know their priority and act to get it done.

While the greats know precisely where to spend their time, others get distracted by the noise. Some focus on the perceived urgent instead of learning and crushing the essentials. Some confuse busyness with productivity and have become averse to the word "No." So many of us want to be perceived as a go-getter who can always get things done, so we say yes to everything. You may have been taught from an early age that if you want something done right, do it yourself. That it is faster if you do it yourself. Most recently, this "you are enough" mantra has been so ingrained that many believe something must be wrong if we ask for help. But these are all distractions. No one is enough to do everything; no one has all the answers, we can't do everything now. When we try to do it all, our actions have no clarity; we waste a ton of time and expend all our energy for truly little return.

For many of us, our feelings become distractions. We justify our feelings, and if we don't want to do something, don't like something, or don't feel like it, then it must be the wrong thing to do. Here's the thing: our feelings are distractions. If you want to be successful, then you must check your feelings at the door.

For instance, parents never feel like changing their child's blow-out diaper, yet they do. They don't want to do it and don't enjoy it. They just do it. Why? Because that is their job, that is their responsibility, it is something required of reliable parents, and being a good parent is the priority.

Many healthy people exercise before the sun comes up. Though some have grown to enjoy this time, that probably wasn't always the case and isn't the case for many. Fun is not the point of an early morning workout routine, though it can be a byproduct. Those who exercise in the morning do it because being fit is a priority. They get it done, like it or not, because it's the only time it fits into their schedule.

Often, at work or in my coaching career, I had to do things I didn't enjoy and didn't want to, but I got them done anyway. Some issues arose: conflicts that needed to be addressed, individuals that needed to be let go, and cuts that needed to be made. I can tell you that there was not one time that I wanted to do any of these things, but that didn't matter. It was what was required, and I was the one responsible for doing it. Being a great coach was a priority for me.

We fail to become as significant as possible because so many of us get distracted by our feelings. We get our feelings hurt because it is hard, because we are not perfect, or because someone wasn't kind, so we quit and are then left with nothing but what-ifs, should-haves, could-haves, and would-haves. Therein lies the distraction. We allow our feelings to impact our responsibilities. We allow our emotions to dictate our actions, and these excuses prevent us from becoming our best.

People fail not because they lack desire, as we all want to be healthy, have a great family, and be productive. It's the lack of productive action that prevents many from being successful.

I have yet to meet a person who wakes up to be average. None of us wake up and think, "Today, I just want to get by." No, we all wake up wanting to be great. Yet so many of us have no idea how to start our days or what we need to do to make the day great. And this lack of clarity causes us to sleep until the last possible moment, which wrecks everything. Instead of getting up and doing something productive like exercising, reading, or just pausing to remember how grateful we are, we hit snooze. Then we are rushed and late. We jump out of bed and immediately race around the house, trying to prepare for work. We hurry our kids up and rush them to get dressed for school. We're desperately looking for homework, water bottles, and shoes. Trying to make lunches and frantically yelling for everyone to hurry. Then, we throw some junk food down our children's mouths, push them out of the house, and practically kick them out of the car door as we drop them off for school and speed to work.

Just like that, the morning is over, and your kids are gone, yet you failed to do anything productive. You didn't create one positive memory, have one great conversation, or do one thing of value, and this failure causes immediate regret. Your day could have gotten off to a fantastic start if you had set your priorities, knew what you were supposed to do, and had the discipline to get it done. Your morning should have been a success.

But it wasn't, and now you feel unsuccessful and stressed out. Then you show up to work. Once again, you want to be successful and make an impact but don't fully know what to do to succeed. So, you do stuff. You check a lot of emails, respond to a bunch of clients, upload useless information to your CRM, and jump from meeting to meeting to meeting. Then the workday is over, yet you can't recall one thing of value that you completed. You didn't stop moving the entire day, yet you can't think of one positive impact you made, and this lack of productivity causes you to question the purpose of your work.

Some people show up to work, bust their tails, and believe that they are crushing it. Unfortunately, they have become great at unimportant tasks—the wrong things—and this distraction has convinced them that they need only to work harder. However, doing more of the wrong things does not lead to success. It leads to more frustration, guilt, regret, and burnout.

For instance, families want to be great, and some parents convince themselves that making a lot of money is the most important thing they can do to provide for their family, regardless of how many hours they must put in. I'm not saying that making money and providing is bad, as this is important and honorable. I'm highlighting that some parents believe giving money is their main responsibility. They are great at providing income but are awful at having meaningful conversations with their kids. These parents don't know their kids' friends, don't know what's going on in their children's lives, and rarely spend time with them. These parents are doing a lot of stuff but have become great at the wrong things, and the distraction of primarily being the provider is wrecking their relationships.

CEOs, high-level coaches, and leaders can perform well and make sound decisions. In fact, their ability to consistently perform and make significant decisions has led to many of their achievements and helped them be promoted. Yet, at the same time, these tremendous performers are sometimes awful at teaching others how to perform or make similar decisions. Because they can't teach or coach, they must make every decision or do everything themselves, leading to burnout and massive turnover.

Inversely, I've worked with and seen people who can teach but don't perform. They might teach someone how to lead but can't lead themselves. They can preach the Gospels but don't apply them in their own lives. I know several people who give sound advice on relationships, life, finances, and health. Yet these same people are awful at implementing any of it.

Just because you know what to do means nothing if you can't or don't implement it. Just because you are great at some things means nothing unless these things are the right things. If you become distracted by the wrong actions, you're destined to fail and live a life of regret.

> **JUST BECAUSE YOU KNOW WHAT TO DO MEANS NOTHING IF YOU CAN'T OR DON'T IMPLEMENT IT.**

## WHAT EXCUSES ARE YOU ALLOWING TO HOLD YOU BACK?

## WHAT ARE THE DISTRACTIONS THAT KEEP YOU FROM BEING PRODUCTIVE?

Create a plan so that you have successful mornings and productive days.

## WHAT TIME DO YOU NEED TO GET UP?

## WHAT CAN YOU GET PREPARED FOR YOUR DAY THE NIGHT BEFORE?

Aside from our feelings, many people will use time as an excuse. They convince themselves they don't have enough time, it's not the right time, or they'll do it tomorrow. This arrogant thinking is destructive because none of us are promised tomorrow. None of us know how much time we have left. If you wait till tomorrow to do what should have been done today, you're greatly limiting your chances of success.

Let's be honest. Do you see fit people waiting until next week to work out, or do they just work out? Do you see the best realtors waiting for interest rates to drop before they sell a property, or do they keep selling homes?

Did you see Elon Musk wait for Twitter to go on sale in 2022 before he bought it, or did he just buy it? The bottom line is that the greats just get it done. They know the priority, understand what productivity looks like, and then they do it, no matter what.

Some people are distracted by the idea of balance. They strive and seek a balanced life. Here's the thing: Success isn't about balance. It's not attempting to give the same amount of energy to every aspect of our lives daily. Success is about rhythm. It's about knowing the priority today, consistently getting that thing done, and then allowing everything else to fall in place. We have seasons in life. Seasons when we must spend more time at work, seasons when we should spend more time with family, and all sorts of other seasons that will require different kinds of attention. Balance is flat, equal, and requires the

**SUCCESS ISN'T ABOUT BALANCE. SUCCESS IS ABOUT RHYTHM.**

same amount of time and energy in every aspect of life. Though you may think you want this, you most likely don't, nor is it possible to achieve. My good friend, author, speaker, and mentor, Coach Darleen Santore, compares rhythm to being hooked up to a heart monitor. You don't want to see a flat line if you're hooked up to a heart monitor. A flat line means you're dead. A flat line is balanced. Instead, you want to see ups and downs, spikes and plunges. This shows that your heart is beating and that you are alive. She equates the beat to a rhythm of life. It illustrates a growing sense of responsibility in certain areas, during certain seasons, getting close to a redline, and then needing to let go of some responsibility. Then, we may be ready to take on more responsibilities in a different area of life and spend energy there until we must start saying no and begin delegating again.

You will burn out if you don't know your rhythm, don't know the priority of this season, seek balance, or confuse everything as essential. It's just not possible to do it all well all the time. You'll flatline or operate in the red and not be able to sustain your life.

## WHERE DO YOU NEED TO START SAYING NO AT THIS STAGE OF LIFE?

## IN WHAT AREAS HAVE YOU BEEN SEEKING BALANCE INSTEAD OF FINDING YOUR RHYTHM?

The last distraction that I have found that causes so many of us to fail is that we don't finish. We have a great morning and a good afternoon, and then believe this gives us the right to waste the evening. People will have a tremendous Monday and Tuesday, an okay Wednesday and Thursday, and then hardly show up from Friday to Sunday. Companies will crush Q1 and Q2, have a mediocre Q3, and coast through Q4. The inability to finish distracts us from success. The greats know that how they finish is crucial. Endings are unavoidable, but finishing is intentional; it is a choice of how you finish. The greats know that the game will end, the quarter will end, the meeting will end, the day, week, month, and our lives will eventually end. And they know how they choose to finish these things will greatly impact their legacy.

**ENDINGS ARE UNAVOIDABLE, BUT FINISHING IS INTENTIONAL.**

Just think about how many football games are won or lost in the fourth quarter. One team may have total control through the first three-quarters of the game, but instead of keeping up the intensity, they let up, play as though not to lose, and end up getting dominated in the fourth quarter.

Many marriages start with so much strength and passion, but instead of each partner continuing to invest in that strength, they become complacent and take the relationship for granted. This inability to give effort until the end causes many marriages to end in divorce.

Many people retire, and instead of continuing to grow, they just get old. They don't develop, learn new things, or experience the world. They just get set in their ways and appear to live as if they are waiting to die.

Notable companies figured out a product or service that worked, and instead of continuing to grow, adapt, or improve, they became set in their ways and refused to change. Their inability to adapt and continue to put in the work and finish caused massive companies like Blockbuster, Toys "R" Us, Sears, and many others to ultimately fail.

## WHERE DO YOU NEED TO FINISH?

## WHERE HAVE YOU BECOME SET IN YOUR WAYS?

STAGE THREE: TAKE ACTION
# CHAPTER 11: THE GREATS' ACTIONS

*Greatness is open to all but earned by few!*
**Darleen Santore**

If you want to be successful, you must make a plan, execute that plan, and tweak it when needed. Success is ensuring that the end goal is entirely within your control and then taking the necessary steps to get there. The greats understand that they will eventually achieve all their dreams; they just can't achieve them all now. The greats know they need to seek constant feedback, or they will ultimately become stagnant or do the wrong things.

For instance, John Wooden had a four-step process to success.

First, he set his plan daily and ensured that he, his coaches, players, wife, and children knew the plan. He ensured practice, meetings, and events were effectively and efficiently executed. (Impelman, 23)

## HOW DO YOU PLAN OUT YOUR DAY?

## HOW MUCH TIME DO YOU WASTE WHEN YOU DO NOT PLAN YOUR DAY?

## WHAT IS THE MOST PRODUCTIVE THING YOU CAN DO TODAY?

What one action will give you the best return on your investment?

Second, John Wooden had everything prepared before practice or before the day began. He made sure the court was set up how he needed it and that they had plenty of basketballs, tape, shoelaces, water, or anything else the team might need to run an effective practice. He ensured his house was in order and knew where everything was before bed. (Impelman, 23)

## HOW MUCH TIME IS WASTED WHEN YOU OR YOUR TEAM AREN'T PREPARED OR ORGANIZED FOR THE DAY?

Third, he maximized the use of time by ensuring that almost every drill practiced multiple fundamentals. Regardless of his players' skill levels, they were constantly passing, rebounding, moving, and cutting without the ball. (Impelman, 23)

Most every game in life is won or lost because of fundamentals. Whoever can block, line up, and tackle the best tends to win the football game. Whichever couple continues to build trust with one another tends to last. Whichever companies know and live by their values tend to have amazing and long-lasting companies. Why? Because they focus on the fundamentals.

## WHAT ARE THE FUNDAMENTALS OF YOUR BUSINESS, RELATIONSHIPS, AND PERSONAL LIFE?

## HOW OFTEN ARE YOU WORKING ON THE FUNDAMENTALS?

Finally, Coach Wooden would analyze the practice immediately. He and his staff would review the practice, see what needed to be tweaked and adjusted, plan to refocus in a new area, and then make the appropriate adjustments. (Impelman, 23)

It's incredible how little we reflect on the day. Few of us take the time to review if what we're doing is working, if it's being done the right way, or how we can improve it. This lack of information causes many of us to fail.

## WHEN WAS THE LAST TIME YOU SOUGHT FEEDBACK?

## WHO IS COACHING YOU TO IMPROVE AND ENSURING YOU'RE DOING WHAT YOU SAY?

## WHO CAN YOU CONTACT AND ASK TO PROVIDE YOU WITH COACHING AND ACCOUNTABILITY?

How does Richard Branson oversee forty companies with thousands of employees, invest in his relationships and hobbies, connect with God, read books, and partake in philanthropy? He doesn't.

What I mean is that he doesn't do all of this himself. No one can oversee forty companies with thousands of employees and account for billions of dollars.

Richard Branson hires a team of amazing people and then lets them run. He doesn't micromanage or ensure that everything is done his way. He hires tremendous individuals who are often more competent and qualified than he is, and then he lets them do their thing. This way, he can focus on the more significant priorities. He didn't want to build a large business that eventually consumed him and prevented him from doing what he loved. He wanted to create something great that would allow him to be happy and not overwhelmed. (Haden, 23)

How often do we see people overwhelmed? They start a business, climb the ladder, and double the size of their company, only to create something so big that it consumes their every waking moment and harms all other areas of their lives.

When I was first hired as a head baseball coach, I wanted to do it all. I wanted to be involved in every decision, know everything that was going on, and ensure everything was done my way. This was exhausting and not productive. Eventually, I received tremendous advice from a trusted mentor, Thornton Kipper, who said, "Brandon, let your coaches coach."

**LET YOUR COACHES COACH.**

No one decides to become a coach in hopes of sitting on a bucket and watching someone else coach. No coach shows up to share their knowledge with players, hoping someone else will tell them what to say and how to do things.

Hire knowledgeable and capable people, then let them go. Trust them to do a good job. This has been some of the best advice I have ever received because it has allowed me to do multiple things, be accomplished, lead massive teams, and not burn myself out.

Most of the obstacles we face in life are not actually what is holding us back from success. It's usually our reaction to the obstacle that causes our problems. It's how we attempt to carry the weight of the issue that crushes us. As a visual, have you ever held a baby in your arms for an extended period of time? Even a tiny, seven-pound, precious bundle of joy will eventually wear out even the most enormous biceps. But if you put that baby in a child's backpack or Baby Björn, anyone could carry her all day.

If I were to put 400 pounds on a barbell, I could not bench press or squat it, but I could deadlift it several times. Why? Because I chose to carry the weight differently. It wasn't the weight that was the problem; it was how I chose to carry that weight that created the issue.

Richard Branson and the other greats don't try to handle the weight by themselves. Instead, they always look for more efficient and effective ways to address any issue. Like John Wooden, Richard Branson is always seeking feedback from every level of employee on what they are doing and how they can do it better.

Many of the greats ask themselves and their teams a few questions. These questions ensure that they are productive instead of merely busy.

## THE GREATS ASK, "AM I DOING THE RIGHT THINGS?"

As highlighted in the previous chapter, it's amazing how many of us confuse being in motion with productive action. We confuse busyness with productivity. Just because you're running around all day means nothing unless you're doing the right things. I've coached and been around baseball for over 40 years and know that if you don't have the fundamentals of throwing, catching, and hitting, the game will be challenging for you. However, I see so many coaches and teams neglecting these three aspects. Instead of working on the fundamentals, they spend countless hours putting in special bunt defenses, trick pick-off plays, and unique 1st-3rd defenses. These things are fun and might work once a year, but it's not a great use of their time and effort. If their teams can't field a routine groundball, catch a fly ball, or put the ball in play, the chance of winning many games is very low. Their teams are working hard, but they aren't working smart. I use the majority of practice making sure my players can throw, field, and absolutely mash baseballs. We tended to win many games because we worked on the things that gave us the most significant return on our investment.

## ARE YOU DOING THE RIGHT THINGS, AND HOW DO YOU KNOW?

WHAT ARE THE FUNDAMENTALS OF YOUR JOB?


WHAT ARE THE FUNDAMENTALS FOR STRONG RELATIONSHIPS?


WHAT ACTIVITIES ARE YOU DOING THAT ARE JUST BUSY WORK?


WHO ARE YOU MICROMANAGING?


WHAT TASKS CAN YOU DELEGATE TO SOMEONE ELSE?


ARE YOU SEEING THE RETURN YOU WANT FROM THE TIME YOU INVEST IN YOUR WORK, FAMILY, AND PERSONAL LIFE?


ARE YOU NOTICING YOUR RELATIONSHIPS IMPROVING, YOUR HEALTH GETTING BETTER, OR A REDUCTION IN STRESS?

If not, then there is a good chance you aren't doing the right things.

## WHAT IS YOUR PLAN TO ENSURE YOU ARE DOING PRODUCTIVE ACTIVITIES STARTING NOW?

## THE GREATS ALSO ASK, "AM I DOING THINGS THE RIGHT WAY?".

The Greats want to guarantee that they behave ethically and morally and that their quality is top-notch. If not, they could be wasting time and making destructive decisions. For instance, my company consistently posts social media content every week, but we aren't gaining the followers and views we are hoping for. We are doing the right things but obviously not doing them the right way because we are not getting the return we seek. We aim to positively impact as many people as possible, so we must adjust and find a better way. Someone can be winning the most games, landing the most deals, climbing the corporate ladder, or selling the most books, but if they're cheating or behaving unethically to do so, obviously that is not doing it the right way, and they run the risk of destroying their reputation.

## HOW DO YOU ENSURE YOU ARE DOING THINGS ETHICALLY?

## WHAT ARE YOUR VALUES?

## HOW DO YOU WALK THEM OUT SO THEY ARE NOT MERELY WORDS ON A PAGE?

## FINALLY, THE GREATS ASK, " HOW CAN I DO THINGS BETTER?".

The best consistently critique their ideas and seek more productive and creative ways of doing things. They want to provide the most value in the most effective and efficient ways possible. They are always looking to improve and make things better.

## HOW OFTEN ARE YOU SEEKING FEEDBACK ABOUT YOUR WORK?

## HOW OFTEN ARE YOU CHANGING, MODIFYING, OR IMPROVING YOUR PROCESS?

## HOW CAN YOU INNOVATE, GET CREATIVE, TRY SOMETHING NEW, OR HIRE SOMEONE TO HELP YOU PRESENT YOUR IDEA, PRODUCT, OR SERVICE BETTER WITH MORE EFFICIENCY?

When you study the greats, you realize their success didn't happen accidentally. They didn't wake up one morning and magically have six-pack abs, a massive portfolio, or create a beautiful family. They were intentional with everything they did. They had a plan, knew the goal, executed it, and then constantly adjusted it to improve. If something didn't make sense or whatever they were doing wasn't working or was a waste of time, they stopped doing it. If it was not making them, their company, relationships, or their health better, then it was a distraction and cut out of their life.

Think about how productive you could be if you cut the time-wasting activities out of your life. As mentioned, time is finite. We only get so much of it, and none of us know how much we will get. Whenever we scroll through social media, binge-watch Netflix, sit in a meeting, take that sales call, hit the gym, or go on a date, we exchange our life for that event. As this is the case, you had better get something out of it because you are sacrificing a lot. If not, then why are you doing it?

**THINK ABOUT HOW PRODUCTIVE YOU COULD BE IF YOU CUT THE TIME-WASTING ACTIVITIES OUT OF YOUR LIFE.**

Look at professional football players. In any given season, they will play 17 games; if they are fortunate to make it to the Super Bowl, they will play 19 to 20 games. According to the Wall Street Journal, the average NFL game includes only 11 minutes of actual playing time. At most, a typical player will be a part of only half of those minutes. (Biderman, 10) Think about the amount of focus, sacrifice, detail, preparation, planning, practicing, lifting, running, eating, rehabbing, icing, stretching, and reflecting that goes into those 17-20 games. Every aspect of each day is dialed in all year long so they can have peak performance for less than 110 minutes of playing time. Others of us who are not NFL players must sell, build, construct, litigate, grade, teach, heal, lead, parent, and love hundreds if not thousands of times a year. We must perform at an unprecedented level, yet many of us have no plan for how to accomplish that. We don't practice; we don't prepare; we don't reflect; we don't exercise; we don't rest; we don't rehab; we don't read; we aren't coached; we aren't focused; we aren't prepared; we don't grow. Then, we wonder why our lives are filled with regrets.

The bottom line is that your life is meant to be extraordinary, and you are perfectly designed to enjoy your days, but this requires you to do the things that create an extraordinary and joyful life. Your work is never done. You are never finished. There is always a way to improve your thinking and be more moral, and processes that can be more efficient, changed, or improved. John Wooden didn't wake up one day and think, "Ahh, I've arrived, I'm done." Richard Branson has yet to wake up one morning and decide not to get out of bed, and Derek Jeter hasn't stopped being his persistent, hard-working self because his playing days are over. They always pursue excellence, and their consistent, productive activity ensures they will continue growing.

# WHAT ARE SOME TIME-WASTING ACTIVITIES YOU CAN CUT OUT OF YOUR LIFE?

To close this chapter, I want to share a story that I read from Steve Gilbert, who quoted Trevor Moawad about productive action.

*The late Trevor Moawad used to tell a story about a person his dad met: The son of a single mom, he had just finished his junior year in high school. He failed most of his classes, and his future was not bright. His mom (his father was not in their lives) begged him to take the SAT, and out of respect for her, he took it one morning.*

*When he got his test result in the mail, he was stunned: 1,480.*

*That's 1,480 out of a possible 1,600 -- a tremendous score.*

*His mother asked if he cheated, and he told her he would have, but there was no way for him to do so.*

*Come his senior year, he started going to class and hanging around some of the more academically accomplished students. He ended up graduating, going to a community college, and then Wichita State University, and he became a very successful entrepreneur.*

*Twelve years later, he received a letter in the mail from Princeton, NJ, where the SAT is based. They will audit scores over time, and it turns out his test had been graded wrong. He actually got a 740 out of 1,600.*

*Trevor Moawad's dad wanted his son to get this message from the story: What made the difference for this kid was that in his senior year, he thought he was like a 1,480 student and then began behaving like a 1,480 student. He went to class, studied, and prepared.*

*In order to see a change in our circumstances, we need to change our behavior, not our feelings. This individual started acting like a good student before he actually was one.*

*Whatever you aspire to be, ask yourself this question: How does a person who has accomplished or attained what you want act? What behaviors are the key to their success? Then, start incorporating those behaviors into your life little by little. Eventually, your feelings will catch up to your behaviors.*
*Steve Gilbert*

## STAGE THREE: TAKE ACTION
# CHAPTER 12: HOW TO BE PRODUCTIVE

*"If you commit to nothing, you'll be distracted by everything."*
**James Clear**

What does productivity look like to you? What are the one to two things that, when you do them, make your day awesome? What are those one to two actions that, when done, have the biggest impact on your personal and professional life, finances, health, mindset, faith, and relationships?

Maybe a better place to start is to figure out the biggest distractions in your life. What's the biggest waste of your time? Who or what is taking up too much of your time and not providing anything in return? Is it social media or television? Is it your negative attitude or lack of confidence? Is it mediocre quality at work, drama within the office, or a narcissistic boss? Is it a lack of resources, money, or skill?

Figuring out what is productive or discovering what is a distraction takes intentionality. You must be focused on what you are doing and then reflect on your outcomes. Are the actions you're taking giving you the results that you seek? Are you getting the most significant returns on your investments? Often, this can be a trial-by-error process. You will try something; it won't work, and you continue trying new things until you figure out what does work. For instance, I have tried many different types of fitness programs throughout my life. In all my efforts, I have found that my body responds the best to CrossFit. Participating in one-hour CrossFit workouts four to five times a week is the most effective way to increase my level of fitness. In business, I have learned that meeting with ten different decision-makers weekly is the best thing I can do to grow my client base, provided my mission for each meeting is to bring value to the leader. Doing this consistently has been the most effective action I have found to grow my business.

If you need guidance on setting priorities correctly, observing successful leaders can provide great insight. If you want to be better at sales, notice the activities the best salesperson is doing throughout his day. If you want to improve your marriage, learn what happy couples are doing consistently to make their marriage strong. Observe how top-notch leaders interact with their people, make decisions, or handle conflict. Then, consider implementing some of their strategies. Begin to find the ones that work best for you, consistently perform them, and then work to improve.

The most effective way I have seen people find their one to two productive daily actions is through proper goal setting. Goals are essential. If you

**CLARITY CREATES URGENCY.**

don't have them, you have no clear direction and will be distracted by everything. Goals keep us focused, let us know where we are going, and help us measure our progress. Unfortunately, many of us don't set proper goals, which impacts our ability to have clear priorities. When you know what you are supposed to do and when you are supposed to do it, it is much more likely to get done. Why? Because clarity creates urgency. When you know the focus, the purpose, and the action that needs to be taken, that goal is as sure as done. If you want to ensure that you're headed in the right direction and that your goals provide this productive clarity, then take these three steps to set your goals.

## GOAL SETTING STEP ONE: SET THE APPROPRIATE NUMBER OF GOALS

It's crazy how many people, companies, and teams I see set an outrageous number of goals and others who set none. In both scenarios, no clarity is provided, which usually leads to failure. You only have so much time, money, energy, and capital, so you cannot do everything now. When you take on too many priorities, you will be good at some, great at none, and quit most. Attempting to do too much all at once will rob you of greatness. I'm not saying that you can't do them all; you just can't do them all now.

For instance, when I was an educator, I remember being given three district goals, three school goals, three department goals, three subject goals, and three personal goals every year. I was responsible for fifteen new goals each school year on top of all my other responsibilities. These unrealistic expectations led to stress that overwhelmed me and most of my colleagues. No person can make and lead fifteen new goals in one year. Because of the bogus expectations and feeling over-whelmed, many teachers would boycott these goals altogether, continue doing things the way they had always done, and fail to improve at all.

Great companies and successful people don't do this. They choose an appro-priate number of meaningful goals that push their employees past their comfort zone. Great leaders don't overwhelm their people or themselves with fifteen goals a year or change their minds after only a few months. They set a few impactful goals and then create a plan to reach them. These goals are difficult and require a lot of effort and energy. But because there are few, because they are consistently talked about and monitored, they can manage them, invest in them, and give them the chance to be accomplished.

On the other end of the spectrum, some companies and individuals don't have any goals. They aren't seeking to improve anywhere. If this is you, then what's the point of showing up each day? If you aren't seeking to improve, learn, and grow, you will be irrelevant very soon.

I have worked with many people who are masters at consistently creating and achieving amazing goals within their professional lives, yet haven't set a single personal or family goal in years. These accomplished leaders will spend weeks strategically planning their professional year, revisiting values, and focusing on a plan for rewarding and achieving their professional goals. Then, these same leaders go home without family values, plans, direction, or goals, and they wonder why their lives are out of rhythm. They wonder why it is so hard to find time to spend with their family. Where's the happiness, the excitement, and the fun if you don't have anything to look forward to? What's the future likely to look like if you don't build a plan to create it?

Building a successful family life is more important than your professional life. You should be extra intentional when planning your home life goals. Be specific about what you want and how you will build time and activities to achieve your family goals.

## WHAT ARE YOUR CURRENT GOALS?
### PROFESSIONAL –


### PERSONAL –


### RELATIONAL –


## HOW MANY CAN YOU SUCCESSFULLY MANAGE AND ACHIEVE?


I'm not going to tell you how many goals you should have, as we all have different capacities and resources, but for me and my company, Infinite Strengths, we do one goal a year. Why? Because there are just two of us, we don't have the time, energy, or resources to focus on and execute more than one new goal. For instance, in our first year of business, our goal was to get our Leadership Maximization Program up and running. We wanted to create it in a way we were proud of and then begin taking as many people as possible through it. In year 2, we added a continuation program called "GRIT." This allowed us to continue working with some amazing clients yearly. In year three, we built a virtual mastermind program called The Standard. We began hosting a leadership summit at the end of year three and into year four. Now, in year five, we are writing this book. We could not have achieved all five of these goals in year one. We would have burnt ourselves out and created subpar programs, and our business would have failed quickly. But we figured out that we can take on one goal a year, build it the right way, and continue growing at a sustainable pace.

Virgin and Richard Branson, on the other hand, have billions of dollars and thousands of employees. They can take on a heck of a lot more yearly goals than Infinite Strengths. I don't care what your number is, so long as you do them and have the resources to do them well. I believe it is better to have one goal and crush it instead of setting five goals and only accomplishing one.

## GOAL SETTING STEP TWO: FIND A STRONG 'WHY' BEHIND EACH GOAL

Often, we create a goal without a strong purpose. We set a goal because we hear many other people are doing it. We take on a new initiative because our competitors are doing the same thing. We attempt to do something new because we read about it in a book, and it seemed like a good thing to try. But here's the thing: if there's no strong 'Why,' all we'll do is 'try.' We will start it, and then, when it gets complicated, we will quit and pat ourselves on the back because we tried.

Did you know that 95% of people will quit their New Year resolutions by the 2nd week of January? (Robbins, 23)

Think about that. Ninety-five percent of the people who set out to improve in some area of their lives quit (almost immediately). I believe this is because they don't really know why they are doing it. It's a goal they know they should go after. It's something that would be good for them, but good isn't a strong enough reason for most people to make uncomfortable changes. People aren't willing to sacrifice and change for the long haul. We all know eating healthy benefits us, but that isn't a strong enough reason to make many of us pass on the cookies or bacon for more than a week or two. We all know that exercise is important and that we

**GOOD IS THE BIGGEST THIEF OF GREAT.**

feel better when we do it, but once again, life gets in the way; many people's purposes aren't strong enough, and they quit after a couple of workouts. People are rarely willing to dig deeper for their "why." Change is hard when we don't have a strong purpose pushing us through. Companies know that they need to increase sales, improve their culture, train their team, or diversify their clientele, and these are all good changes, but good is the biggest thief of great.

I want you to go three whys deep on each of your goals to find your true purpose. I want you to keep asking and answering why until you have asked and answered three times. Your 'why' isn't strong enough if you can't get there. You won't have the resolve to keep going. But, when you can get to that third why, you've usually found a selfless reason to keep going. You've generally gotten to a place where you realize that your goal isn't really about you but how you can be there for other people or how this goal can improve other's lives. When we know people are counting on us, it is way less likely we will stop. We will find a way to get things done, regardless of the sacrifice, because we know people are depending on us.

For instance, I was coaching a woman who had gone through a rough patch in her life. She had started drinking way too much, spent some time in jail, and even had her kids taken away from her. Several factors led up to this, but we won't go into that here. We will, however, talk about her response to this situation and her goal. While I was mentoring her, she worked a couple of jobs and was very negative. She was complaining about the work, the hours, and the people. She was just exhausted. Her productivity was lagging; she consistently showed up late, and she was about to lose one job if things didn't change soon.

She was working two jobs, but why? Why was she doing this? Her first answer was all about the money. Well, if you're only working for the money, then regardless of what you're doing, that job will become stagnant, boring, and a drain soon. I asked again, why the money? Why did she need it? Her second answer was that she wanted to own her own place. She was currently living in a community home with other women battling addiction, and she wanted her own place. This was much better than her first reason, but her why still only dealt with her, and she already had a place to lay her head. Whether or not she made any more money, her need for lodging was met. I then asked, why the home? She already had a place to live, so why was having her own home important? Eventually, she got to her strong and mighty Why! She realized she wasn't working these jobs for the money or a home but it was to be reunited with her kids. Her kids wanted to be with her, and she wanted to be with them, but the state would only reinstate custody if she had a stable home and could show that she was paying bills and being a responsible citizen. She wasn't working two jobs for money or a home; she was working two jobs so she could be with her children. She needed no more motivation once she realized the jobs weren't about her. It didn't matter how tired she was or how much she disliked who she worked with; the job wasn't just some job; it was part of the foundation to get her children. Once she uncovered her true purpose, her productivity increased; she was more efficient and pleasant, was always on time, and eventually got a promotion, which allowed her to quit one of her jobs. After several months, she got her own place, showed stability, and was reunited with her children!

Unfortunately, so many of us stop at that first why. We want to increase sales to make more profit; we go to the gym to get healthy; we want a house because it will make us feel better. Though these are all good reasons,

**WHEN YOU FIND THE SELFLESS REASON, YOU WON'T QUIT.**

they aren't strong enough to keep us going when times get hard or we don't want to do them. However, when you find the selfless reason, you won't quit. Read the quick story below, and you decide who has the strongest why. Who has the motivation to keep going, regardless of what life throws at them?

> *Three bricklayers are asked, "What are you doing?" The first says, "I am laying bricks." The second says, "I am building a church." The third says, "I am building the house of God." The first bricklayer has a job, the second has a career, and the third has a calling.*
> *Author, "Unknown"*

Before we move on to the third step to making great goals, I want you to look at your goals and go three whys deep. If you can't get to that third why, then the goal is either wrong or you haven't discovered its true purpose.

## GOAL SETTING STEP THREE: ENSURE THE GOALS ARE TOTALLY WITHIN YOUR CONTROL

Often, this isn't the case. Most people set goals to be the best, to be a career 300-hitter, to be a first-round draft pick, to win a championship, double sales numbers, drop 40 pounds, get married, or become a millionaire. Though admirable, these aren't great goals. Why? Because we don't have complete control over them. Lack of control creates pressure, leaving us feeling like failures if we don't get there.

For instance, I can't force a customer to buy from me; I can't control the market or influence interest rates. I have no say in my opponent's talent or how fast or strong they are. As a baseball player, I might have a great day and crush every ball pitched to me, but if I happen to hit the ball directly to a player on the other team and he catches it, I don't get a hit. I can be intentional in my marriage, but if my wife decides she no longer wants to be with me, I can't control her action of ending the marriage. My kids, who are growing into incredibly moral and sound adults, could end up marrying someone with values different from those we taught them, and their values could change. If your goals are attempting to regulate factors outside of your control, then you are setting yourself up for failure, to be depressed, stressed out, and ultimately creating a life of regrets.

A more significant concern with setting goals outside of your control isn't that you could end up feeling like a failure but that you might do whatever it takes to achieve your goals so that you don't fail —even if that means you must do something unethical, illegal, or cheat, to achieve them.

Just recall the College Admissions Scandal in 2019, when celebrity parents fabricated stories of their children's involvement in certain sports so their kids could get into a prestigious University. The goal was to get their kids into the school, and instead of having their child earn a spot, these parents illegally manipulated the system, resulting in jail time and tarnished reputations. Don't get me wrong, I want my children to be successful, and I do all I can to help them, but their achievements will happen because of how hard they worked. Their life outcomes will result from their efforts, not because of my efforts or manipulation.

Goals are often set based on achievements. It's not that achieving is bad; it's that it can have such a major impact on how many of us define our worth. Accomplishments often define our financial worth, our image, our power, and our influence, and we become distracted by their appeal. So, to reach our goals, we sacrifice everything: our values, families, and reputations, and then what is it all for?

Let's take marriage as an example. Many little girls grow up dreaming about their wedding day. So many of the princess movies glorified in our homes depict young ladies finding their prince charming, getting married, and living happily ever after. At a young age, marriage for many girls and boys becomes a goal. They feel it is what they are supposed to do. So, young couples date and then try to "do marriage." But the expectation of getting married is the distraction: marriage isn't something you do; a true marriage is something that happens because two people grow to love one another, are committed to continually investing in one another, and stick it out through the good times and bad. Having a great marriage becomes the byproduct of their commitment. Once you've fallen in love, the goal should be to make the sacrifices necessary to continue growing and valuing each other every day for the rest of your lives. If both people in every marriage had this goal, there would be far less divorce and dysfunction.

I know a couple who dated for several years, were in their late 20s, and figured that they should either get married or break up. If this is your situation, don't get married! It should never be an ultimatum or just a step you feel you are supposed to take.

If the goal of life is to get married, have a family, and live in a stable home, what happens once you have it? Many people lose interest, and the relationship becomes stale. They've already achieved their life goals by their mid-40s yet have another 40-50 years left to live and have nothing to look forward to. Once again, a great marriage is an awesome expectation. Still, the goal resides in the work, in the daily focus of committing to a relationship and pouring into the other person. A great marriage becomes the result of our goal to be a great spouse and the willingness to put in the work to create a relationship that improves with age.

On top of this, creating goals outside our control robs us of joy that should be experienced as part of the journey. Take a major league baseball player, for example. If someone is fortunate enough to play just one game in the 'Bigs,' that makes him one of only 20,532 people to have ever accomplished this feat. (Baseball Almanac, 24)

Yet many major leaguers believe they are a failure because they struck out too many times, didn't get enough hits, didn't play long enough, failed to become an all-star, or never signed a big contract. Seriously? They're one of the very few to reach the world's most elite level of baseball. They've sacrificed, worked, and committed their whole life to become the best they could be, yet because they didn't get a hit, gave up a home run, or were let go, they somehow weren't successful. If that's the case, then how many hits must one get to be considered a success? How many years must one play in the major leagues to be considered successful? No one can calculate this because these accomplishments have nothing to do with success.

The goal is preparation. It's about the work that has been done, the discipline, the adjustments made, and the effort put forth in studying the opponent, the material, or the information. The goal is the mindset of staying focused on the now, not allowing the past to dictate the present or having the future distract him from the moment. When this is the goal and the person has done the work to back it up, he is successful, regardless of what happens in the at-bat, the presentation, the event, the test, or the day.

## ARE YOUR GOALS BASED MORE ON OUTCOMES OR THE PROCESS?
## GOALS WITHIN YOUR CONTROL

- make ten sales calls each day.
- go to the gym four times a week.
- have a date night with your spouse every week.

## GOALS NOT FULLY WITHIN YOUR CONTROL

- become the top salesperson in the company.
- lose 50 pounds.
- have a perfect marriage.

## ARE YOUR GOALS WITHIN YOUR CONTROL?

## HOW DO YOU ENSURE YOU'RE DOING THE RIGHT THINGS THE RIGHT WAY AND SEEKING TO DO THEM BETTER?

## HOW DO YOU CREATE THE DISCIPLINE TO DO WHAT YOU SHOULD DO?

The bottom line is that goals are important. They keep you focused and growing and guide your decisions throughout the day. However, they must be the goals that can be achieved by your actions. Goals that you have the power to achieve. To further hammer in this point, I want to emphasize it one more time. Having a goal without action is nothing more than a wish. If you want to live life without regret, then you must act and set goals that are in your control. Talking does nothing; emoting over an issue is pointless, and dreaming amounts to many regrets if you don't act and consistently pursue your goals.

Please visit our Distracted by Success Facebook page and let us know what productivity looks like with you.

www.facebook.com/groups/distractedbysuccess/

# ROAD TO SUCCESS STAGE FOUR:
## BUILD SOMETHING THAT LASTS

# STAGE FOUR: BUILD SOMETHING THAT LASTS
## CHAPTER 13: DISTRACTED BY SELFISH DESIRES

*"The two most important days in life are the day you were born and the day you find out why."*
**Mark Twain**

If you could live your life over again, what would you change? How would you do things differently? What regrets would you be sure to erase?

If you could go back to high school or college, what would you do differently? If you could play your sport again, would you change anything? What if you could return to those first few years of your marriage? Would you treat your spouse differently? What if you could return to your children's infant or toddler years? How would you parent better? What if you could go back to that day, that week, that month, or that year? How would you change?

I love to ponder these questions because the insight we can gain puts so much of life into perspective. Our answers highlight the things that really matter.

For instance, many people I have worked with, who in their younger years ran life as if they were the only ones who mattered, deeply regret their selfish acts.

Men regret their playboy ways, neglecting their children or breaking their wives' hearts.

Women, determined to rise to the top, regret not being there for their children. They feel guilty for not taking enough time for their marriage or failing to take vacations when they could.

Retired people regret not going after their dreams, not taking chances, or not doing what they love. They are disappointed that they allowed their fears to hold them back.

Coaches wish they stopped coaching or at least coached less when their children were young so they wouldn't have missed so much of them growing up.

People wish they had spent more time with their loved ones, made more of the important calls, visited family more frequently, or just wished they had let those who passed know how much they were loved.

A friend of mine, who hadn't been home in many years, went back to attend his grandmother's funeral. When he arrived, his grandfather asked him, "If you weren't going to come home and spend time with your grandmother when she was alive, why are you doing it now? Though this question was harsh, my friend's grandfather had it right. Why do we get so distracted with stuff that we neglect the relationships that mean the most to us?

**WHY DO WE GET SO DISTRACTED WITH STUFF THAT WE NEGLECT THE RELATIONSHIPS THAT MEAN THE MOST TO US?**

When we pause and reflect on what we would do differently, we gain a new perspective and focus on the things that matter. If we heed our own retrospective advice, we can ensure we won't make similar mistakes in the future and can guide those around us from making the same mistakes.

What I have come to realize is that our selfish ambitions are what tend to distract us most. When we become so focused on getting ours and lose sight of those around us, we are destined to make many regretful decisions. This is evident when you read a study completed by gerontologist Karl Pillemer, where he interviewed 1,500 people over 65 and asked them what haunts them most about their life choices. (Pillemer, 19)

These were the top responses.

Not being careful enough when choosing a life partner.

Not resolving a family fight.

> If it's within your power to resolve the fight, do it. Because whatever you fought over when you were 40 isn't worth it when you're 80.

**IF IT'S WITHIN YOUR POWER TO RESOLVE THE FIGHT, DO IT. BECAUSE WHATEVER YOU FOUGHT OVER WHEN YOU WERE 40 ISN'T WORTH IT WHEN YOU'RE 80.**

Putting off saying how you feel

> You can't go back and ask for forgiveness, apologize, express gratitude, or even get information from someone who has died.

Not Traveling enough.

> Experience the world while you can, for you have no idea what tomorrow brings.

Spending too much time worrying.

> Most of the things we fret about never happen, yet we waste days, weeks, months, and even years worrying about them.

Not being honest

> Lying, being deceitful, cheating, having an affair, or being dishonest, and especially dishonesty from others, haunts them.

Not taking enough career chances.

> They regretted the moves they didn't make instead of embracing what they did.

Not taking care of your body.

Not taking care of your body doesn't mean you will die young. It means that you're going to be stuck with 10-20 years of a chronic disease while modern medicine keeps you alive.

You'll notice that none of these regrets revolved around money, power, fame, or winning. They instead highlight the people, experiences, and memories that were neglected because people were distracted by the wrong things. We get distracted by the incorrect goals, put too much emphasis on what others think, worry about the things we cannot control, hold grudges over things that don't really matter, live as if we can do it later, and all the while we miss out on this amazing life.

We selfishly chase the titles, the power, the fame, and the money, believing that these things will provide meaning to our life, only to get them or not, and realize we've been pursuing the wrong road to success all along. We get to the end of our life and realize we missed it. We acquired stuff to leave behind but very few wonderful memories. We gained titles but very few friends. We were promiscuous with several different people but never got to experience the true love that comes with commitment. We got to meet a lot of interesting people but never knew our children. We got promoted and got to experience the world, yet in the end, it cost you and your family dearly.

Interestingly, I can't recall ever feeling regretful for a selfless act. I could be wrong, and you can try to prove this wrong, but it is impossible to ever regret treating someone how you want to be treated.

**IT IS IMPOSSIBLE TO EVER REGRET TREATING SOMEONE HOW YOU WANT TO BE TREATED.**

I've never regretted treating my wife like the most important person in the world. I've never regretted celebrating my children, going above and beyond for a client, helping a neighbor, apologizing for a wrong I had made, calling my grandmother on the phone, visiting friends, volunteering at the church, or helping people figure out how to get back on their feet. I've never regretted making life and career changes that benefited my family.

Yet, I and many that I know regret the times when we've lied, cheated, broken the law, picked our career over family, allowed our pride to get in the way of a relationship or chose the easy way instead of the right way. I have come to realize that there are people out there who know who they are, have the right mindset to deal with the challenges that come their way, and

**UNLESS A PERSON NAILS THE LAST STAGE ON THE ROAD TO SUCCESS, THEY WILL CONTINUE TO BE DISTRACTED BY THE WRONG THINGS, AND THEY WILL SURELY LIVE A LIFE OF REGRET.**

will most certainly do what they say they are going to do. But unless a person nails the last stage on the Road to Success, they will continue to be distracted by the wrong things, and they will surely live a life of regret. They might not realize this until later in life, but when they do, the pain of regret will be more than they can bear.

## WHO ARE YOU DOING EVERYTHING FOR?

## WHAT ARE YOU BUILDING?

DISTRACTED  BY SELFISH DESIRES

# STAGE FOUR: BUILD SOMETHING THAT LASTS
# CHAPTER 14: THE GREATS' LEGACIES

*Love is more precious than gold; if you have enough to spare, you're a millionaire.*
**Chris Stapleton**

Imagine you were in a horrible car accident, and you are standing at the pearly gates talking to God. You are trying to negotiate for 15 extra years of life on Earth. What evidence would you provide to prove you are worthy of the additional time?

Take a minute and reflect on this question. What evidence would you share to justify more time? You can't give the cop-out answer that, "I'm not worthy of more time" or "I would give my time to someone else." Seriously, reflect: what have you built that would justify more time? Take some time and answer it now.

This is a profound question. I bet your answers mostly involved people. I bet you thought about your children, your grandkids, your spouse. I bet you mentioned helping others to be their best, teaching, guiding, or mentoring the less fortunate to rise to their potential. I also bet that none of you stated you deserve more time because of the money you've made, the big home you've built, the number of people you've slept with, your fancy vacations, the companies you've started, or the big promotion you earned.

By answering this question, you unveil what matters. You discover that building something that lasts isn't concerned with the physical. It's building people, creating relationships, and making memories that will last well beyond your years. Building something is more about what you pour into people, not what you get out of people. It's helping others to become better, even if that means they become better than you.

The greats understand what's truly important and don't miss it. They dedicate their lives to developing as many people as possible instead of acquiring as much stuff as possible. The greats are more concerned with a person's

**THE GREATS ARE MORE CONCERNED WITH A PERSON'S SOUL THAN THEIR TALENT.**

soul than their talent. They are more focused on character than results. Building something that lasts doesn't require money, power, or fame; it just requires selfless intent with consistent action. The bottom line is that all of us are capable and meant to develop others; we all desire to build something that lasts. It's just that we get too distracted by our ego and are attracted to immediate gratification, and if we don't get what we want or see results soon enough, we quit, thus failing to reach our potential. Did you know that it took John Wooden 16 years before he won his first championship, and then his teams went on a roll? For 16 years, this great man stuck to the process focused on his efforts, continued to become better daily, poured into his players, and eventually, the wins and championships came. Even after his winning streak began, he still stuck to the process, focused on his efforts, continued to become an even better person, and poured into his players. This rarely happens anymore because people and our society have lost their patience. They want the wins, money, position, and titles, and they want them now. If they don't see it soon enough, a coach is fired, a transition is made, or they just quit. But success doesn't happen overnight. It is built, groomed, and created by consistently doing the right things, doing them the right way, and making yourself and those around you better.

The most outstanding leader I've ever had the chance to work with, be coached by, and see in action for several years is my former high school history teacher and freshman football coach, Jeff Callahan, or "Cali," as we call him. This guy was fresh out of college when he entered my life as my freshman football coach. I was a fifteen-year-old kid who loved sports, loved to work, and couldn't wait to hit someone on the football field. I wanted to be the best I could. I just needed guidance. Luckily, I had Cali. This man showed up every day prepared to attack his responsibilities. He was energized, cared about what he was doing, didn't want to waste our time, had a plan, and held us accountable to that plan. He had a Standard, and our job was to meet that Standard both on and off the football field. It didn't matter what was going on; we knew how we were supposed to behave. At the same time, he handled all his responsibilities with class and respect. He wasn't arrogant; he didn't belittle us or blame us. He led us, coached us, and gave us techniques and strategies to help us become better athletes. He brought the same vigor and excitement into his classroom. His energy inspired me to want to become a US History teacher, just like my hero. All the while, at home Cali loves his wife and three children. He spends time with them, plans trips, focuses on creating memories, and pours his wisdom and energy into his family. This man doesn't have millions of dollars, doesn't live in a mansion, or possesses immense power, but if you were lucky enough to go to Bedford North Lawrence High School, you better believe that this man impacted your life. He showed you the path daily and held you accountable for walking it. This man has built something that will last beyond his time on the field or in the classroom because he understands that life is about people and only about people. When he gets to the end of time and comes face to face with God, there will be no guilt, remorse, and only success. Because if he were asked to justify 15 more years, he would have a lifetime of developing people as clear evidence.

We are here to acquire as much wisdom as we can and then share that wisdom with as many who will listen. We are here to build relationships and create communities where others can be seen, feel valued, and feel safe enough to pursue their dreams. It's

**WE ARE HERE TO ACQUIRE AS MUCH WISDOM AS WE CAN AND THEN SHARE THAT WISDOM WITH AS MANY WHO WILL LISTEN.**

this community that makes life worth living. When you study the greats, you'll see that this is precisely what they did. John Wooden built men of character. He built a loving family and cared for all his relationships, regardless of what they could do for him. He didn't develop people so that they could do more for him. He built leaders because that was the right thing to do.

The greats will do what's right for you, regardless of what you can do for them. I don't care where I am or what's going on; Coach Callahan is always there for me. He was at my wedding, visited me in Arizona, participates in one of my leadership programs, and has a trip planned to see me in Boise. He does all of this because he cares. He doesn't invest in my life so that he can do something for him. I can't increase his salary, I can't help him get promoted, I can't hire him, or get him a job. I am just a former player whom he decided to invest in and who he still leads to this day.

When we feel valued and connected, we feel like we can take on the world, and we feel like we belong. Belonging is what we desperately seek; when people let us in, we have a foundation from which to launch ourselves. We have a community that brings purpose to life.

A book titled; "Blue Zones" has recently been turned into a Netflix Series highlighting little pockets of the world where people live the longest. This fantastic series visits five destinations and explores why so many people live to be over a hundred years old and have an average life span of five to seven years longer than the rest of the world. The author, Dan Buettner, suggests several reasons for this phenomenon, including what types of food people in each place eat, how much they eat, and how much they exercise. The one consistent factor that stood out to me was that these fascinating people have a community to connect with. They have friends who expect to see them tomorrow. They have people waiting for them to show up. They have others counting on them to be there and people around to care for them. The citizens of these five areas feel wanted, have a reason to wake up, and have a strong purpose in life. They are building something that keeps them alive longer. They are not living in isolation, consumed with acquiring things or seeking to gain status. They are waking up, exercising, walking, playing games, eating, breaking bread, creating crafts, and enjoying a glass of wine with other people. This community has them laughing, helping, caring, loving, and simply bringing joy to each other's lives. (Buettner, 10)

The most successful teams, companies, families, and leaders understand that the fundamental fact of life is that it **IS NOT ABOUT YOU**. If you were fortunate enough to play for an incredible team or coach, you have experienced this fact. Just think of all the running, conditioning, weightlifting, and early morning workouts you put yourself through. Sure, you captured the benefits of becoming a stronger athlete, but you did it mainly because you knew your team was counting on you. You sacrificed because you knew your teammates were also sacrificing. You accepted your role, worked to improve, encouraged your teammates, and stayed fully committed because you were a part of a community. When we are proud of what we belong to, we will give more than we thought possible. We will go to levels we didn't know existed because failure isn't an option.

> **THE MOST SUCCESSFUL TEAMS, COMPANIES, FAMILIES, AND LEADERS UNDERSTAND THAT THE FUNDAMENTAL FACT OF LIFE IS THAT IT *IS NOT ABOUT YOU.***

The amazing men and women who have been or are a part of the military are willing to make the ultimate sacrifice, not for the stripes on their uniforms or the accolades they can garner from battle, but for the men or women standing next to them. They are willing to give their all because they are a part of a team and a community that is willing to do the same for them. It's this community, this selflessness that has helped make our military one of the greatest powers in the world.

Unfortunately, too many of us miss this last piece of the success puzzle. Some amazing people know exactly who they are, think differently, and will do what they say, but they aren't building something that lasts. This failure causes them to build massive companies, acquire many assets, achieve crazy status, and build enormous bank accounts, but have no meaningful relationships. They have weak families and no one to share all these amazing things with. They have so much knowledge and so many resources, but they are missing life because they aren't building communities or things that will last. Their isolation is killing them.

According to the Center for Disease Control (Center for Disease Control, 21)

- Social isolation significantly increases a person's risk of premature death from all causes, a risk that may rival those of smoking, obesity, and physical inactivity.
- Social isolation was associated with about a 50% increased risk of dementia.
- Poor social relationships (characterized by social isolation or loneliness) were associated with a 29% increased risk of heart disease and a 32% increased risk of stroke.
- Loneliness was associated with higher rates of depression, anxiety, and suicide.
- Loneliness among heart failure patients was associated with nearly four times increased risk of death, 68% increased risk of hospitalization, and 57% increased risk of emergency department visits.

In addition, the National Academies of Sciences, Engineering, and Medicine (NASEM) reported that more than one-third of adults aged 45 and older feel lonely. (Centers for Disease Control, 21) Think about that. One out of every three adults you see aged 45 or older does not feel like they are part of a team, does not feel like they belong, and does not feel like they are needed. Heck, on January 30th, 2024, ABC News highlighted that San Mateo County became the first in the U.S. to declare loneliness a health emergency. We are destroying our lives by failing to encourage people to be a part of a community. (ABC 7, 24)

If I win the race and don't have people there to celebrate my efforts, then what's the point? If I become the best in my field yet don't share this wisdom with those around me, then what's the point? If I hit the first three stages on the Road to Success yet didn't build something that lasts, it was all for nothing.

But regardless of what has gone on in my life, if I have a friend, a community, a family, or a person who loves me, then I have something more precious than any achievement I could ever accomplish.

## WHAT COMMUNITIES DO YOU BELONG TO?

## WHAT NEW COMMUNITY CAN YOU JOIN?

## WHO CAN YOU SHARE YOUR KNOWLEDGE WITH?

I challenge you to pick someone to mentor with the goal of making them better than you.

## WHAT ARE YOU BUILDING?

## WHAT DO YOU WANT YOUR LEGACY TO BE?

STAGE FOUR: BUILD
SOMETHING THAT LASTS
# CHAPTER 15: HOW TO BUILD SOMETHING SIGNIFICANT

*"Legacy is not leaving something behind for other people. It's leaving something behind in other people."*
**Gary Vaynerchuk**

Building something that lasts is simple, but it isn't easy. It is a constant that is always happening and is never finished. It is never complete because it is based on your entire life.

If you desire to build something that lasts, you must do these three things.

## BUILDING SOMETHING THAT LASTS:

<u>Step One</u> - You must set the Standard and then consistently live by it. You must ensure that you have clearly set and communicated your expectations to everyone involved. Then, you must live by the Standard in everything you do. Everyone must understand why they are doing things, who is doing what, when things are supposed to be done, and where they are going. If you review many of the distractions mentioned in this book, you'll find that most stem from a lack of clarity. If you aren't prepared for the day and don't know what you are supposed to do or

what productivity looks like, then you're destined to be busy instead of productive and most likely fail. To get others to give you their full effort, they must be clear on the true selfless purpose behind their actions. They must really understand why it matters. When you know what you're supposed to do, when things are supposed to be done, and why you're doing it, you'll get to work and won't stop. You'll find a way to meet the goal.

At the same time, if you set the expectation yet are lax in execution, your word means nothing. You have no credibility. People are great imitators. Your people will imitate what they see. This means that you must be worthy of imitation. One of your goals should be to become a leader worth following. If not, then you're not building something solid that

**WHEN YOU KNOW WHAT YOU'RE SUPPOSED TO DO, WHEN THINGS ARE SUPPOSED TO BE DONE, AND WHY YOU'RE DOING IT, YOU'LL GET TO WORK AND WON'T STOP. YOU'LL FIND A WAY TO MEET THE GOAL.**

will last. Your foundation is weak. Being someone worthy of imitation is being someone who knows and lives their values. It's being someone who is the same person, regardless of what's going on around them. If you aren't doing this, you aren't building something that lasts. If you aren't clearly setting and living the expectations, then the foundation you're creating won't hold, and once people start standing on it, it will crumble.

## AS A RECAP, WHAT'S YOUR STANDARD? WHAT ARE YOUR VALUES? ARE YOU LIVING THEM?

## WHAT'S THE MOST PRODUCTIVE THING YOU NEED TO DO TODAY?

## BUILDING SOMETHING THAT LASTS:

**Step Two** –You must teach, not tell. You should guide and mentor those in your care to become their best, even if that means they become better than you. Building something that lasts requires that you provide as much value as you possibly can. It's giving away all your wisdom to those around you so they don't make the same mistakes. Building something that lasts doesn't mean that things are only done your way; it just means that they are done correctly and meet the Standard. Imagine a boss with incredible institutional knowledge who doesn't share it with his employees because he's afraid that giving away all his secrets will make him expendable. Is he building something that lasts? Is he developing his people to be the best that they can possibly be? No! But the Jeff Callahan's, John Wooden's, and Kerry Buck's of the world share everything. They give and provide as much value as possible because they want those around them to succeed, even if that means they become better than the teacher.

> **YOU MUST TEACH, NOT TELL.**

Teaching isn't about making people do things the way you do them. It's providing guidance and then a safe platform to practice, fail, learn, and repeat. Their actions allow learning to take place. Just think of how you learned to do most of what you can do. You didn't learn most of it because someone told you how to do it. Sure, that direction helped, but you learned through action. I can tell my son how to swing a bat and show him how to swing a bat, but the only way he's going to learn and get better is to pick up a bat and swing it. To build something that lasts, we must provide the autonomy our people and families desperately need. Helicoptering over them, correcting every move, and dictating how things are done only builds frustration, resentment, dependency, and crushes motivation. Just recall the number of parent-child relationships that are destroyed because the parent is constantly telling their child how to do things. The child has no independence or autonomy and can never seem to do anything right; micromanagement destroys relationships. Abraham Lincoln is quoted as saying, "*The worst thing you can do for those you love are the things they can and should do for themselves.* "When I started coaching, I wanted all my players to throw, hit, and field like me. Why? Because it worked for me. I was fortunate to play baseball at a high level, so why wouldn't everyone want to field, throw, hit, and catch like me? Unfortunately, this strategy created robots. My players were more concerned with fielding like me than getting the guy out. They were more focused on swinging like me than hitting the ball. By telling them how to play, I was taking away their creativity, the fun, their natural way of moving, and other opportunities to learn from other coaches. Did it matter how my players fielded the ball, swung the bat, or threw, so long as they got the guy out, executed the play, or met the expectation? No, it didn't. After a few years of coaching, I learned this essential leadership aspect. Teach the fundamentals, and then let them go and create. Once I stopped telling my players how to play and gave them the autonomy to find their own ways, their abilities soared. The game became fun again; they brought more energy, and they began to master their positions. The most outstanding teachers, parents, leaders, and coaches are always there as a resource to ensure that something awful doesn't happen, but they let you paint the room, swing the hammer, cut the grass, give the presentation, or meet with the big client. They allow you to do it, learn from your mistakes, grow by struggling through the process, and get better. The best don't tell you what to do; they help you develop and discover the answer yourself.

## WHERE ARE YOU PROVIDING AS MUCH VALUE AS POSSIBLE? HOW ARE YOU INVESTING IN OTHERS?

## WHERE ARE YOU HOLDING BACK KNOWLEDGE BECAUSE YOU FEAR BEING EXPENDABLE?

## ARE YOU TEACHING OR TELLING PEOPLE WHAT TO DO? HOW CAN YOU BECOME MORE OF A TEACHER?

## BUILDING SOMETHING THAT LASTS:

**Step Three** – You must coach and encourage your people. Building something that lasts requires that you see your people doing things right and then tell them you noticed. You must be actively looking for remarkable things being done and then encourage those behaviors. See how tasks are being accomplished and then challenge people to do them better. If we ensure that everyone knows the expectation and then don't recognize the efforts toward the expectation or don't hold ourselves and everyone accountable to the expectation, then we aren't building anything at all. We are all talk and no action. Accountability, coaching, and encouragement are what make it real. Follow-through ensures we are who we say we are, are doing what we are supposed to do, and are always getting better.

Think back again to the tremendous leaders in your life. I'll bet you knew their expectations, saw them live it, and knew that if you didn't do what you said you would do, they would challenge you. Leaders who build something that lasts aren't pushovers; they are not meek or weak. They are firm, they are demanding, and they are, at the same time, empathetic and respectful. If you aren't using your voice to encourage, recognize, challenge, and coach your people to improve, they won't grow, even if you're doing everything else right. From my experience, almost everyone I've met will look for an easy way out, justify their unmet expectations, and be less than their best without someone they respect to hold them accountable. This includes me. But when I know someone is counting on me or will be disappointed if I don't do what I say, guess what? I get it done and am better for it.

Before my last two years of coaching, I read the book, "3-Dimensional Coaching," by Jeff Duke. The book highlights that there are three dimensions to coaching. Level One is the physical level and covers mainly the fundamentals. Level Two is body and mind. It teaches the fundamentals but also includes players' motivations, emotions, and confidence and develops team bonding. Level Three is the level coaches should aim for. It includes all aspects of the first two levels but is also concerned with the athlete's heart. At this level, a coach nurtures a player's values, self-worth, identity, character, and significance. Coaching at this level allows players to not only achieve greatness on the field but also become better humans in all other areas of their lives. (Duke, 14)

A great coach must be all 3, but this last one is where you can build something that lasts. The heart of the athlete is where we build community, develop character, teach values, and care more about the person than their talent. To hit this 3rd dimension, you must be intentional, you must be consistent, and you must give authentic encouragement. To help us reach the 3rd dimension, my coaching staff adopted and implemented a strategy I learned from this book called "Knight Time." Knight Time requires you to invite up a player after practice and smother him with positive affirmations. All other players are required to say reasons as to why this athlete is a great teammate. But with this caveat: the reasons must be about the player's character. Someone can't say they love a player because he can hit home runs, throw 95mph, or run fast. They must talk about things like the athlete's selflessness, passion, dependability, loyalty, care, and friendliness, and no reason can be repeated. Each player and coach must provide a unique characteristic they love about that player. By the end of the session, our players had received positive affirmations from five coaches and 18+ teammates. That champion walked off the field with a new pep in their step, knowing that they were loved, that they were valued, that they mattered, and that they were part of something special. We did this for every player and every coach. The players even began doing it on their own. Why? Because they loved it. They loved being appreciated, they loved encouraging others, and they loved being part of something special. The main thing is that we were building men of character who were committed to becoming their best. Interestingly, during those last two years, we didn't win championships or garner titles, but man, did we build something that will last. These men are now incredible husbands and fathers, employees and bosses, friends and neighbors, and I still have a close relationship with many of them.

Verbally communicating the standard and holding people accountable for it is vital. Just because you know and live by the Standard does not mean others will follow your lead. You will have little influence on those around you knowing and living the Standard unless you intentionally, clearly, and consistently explain the expectations, encourage your people to aim for the Standard, and then hold them accountable to follow through. It's wild how many people claim to be leaders but only lead by example. They don't use their voices to challenge, recognize, or coach those around them to improve. Don't get me wrong, you must lead by example, but if you're not consistently communicating with your team, you're not leading. You're not building something that lasts. Jeff Callahan, John Wooden, Richard Branson, and my wife do things the right way, and you better believe that they recognize and hold their people accountable. You better believe they are encouraging, respectful, and always challenging themselves and their people to improve. Because of this, everyone around them gets better.

If we aren't living by The Standard and intentionally teaching these behaviors to those around us, then who is? If my wife and I aren't living by our family values and intentionally teaching our children to become morally sound men and women, then who will teach them? Society? Their friends? Instagram? TikTok? Or some influencer?

**IF WE AREN'T LIVING BY THE STANDARD AND INTENTIONALLY TEACHING THESE BEHAVIORS TO THOSE AROUND US, THEN WHO IS?**

Many people believe sports are a great vehicle for character building. However, this is only true when the coaches are people of sound moral character who intentionally teach their values to their athletes. When this is not the case, the game will be the influencer. For many, the main objective in sports is to win. If our athletes don't have a coach of strong moral character, sports can create the mindset that it is okay to do whatever it takes to win, regardless of ethics.

For our schools to partner in raising amazing adults, we need teachers with a sound moral character who intentionally teach these characteristics to our students. Otherwise, schools only recognize the top performers, those with the highest GPAs and the best-standardized test scores, creating a performance-driven generation. This false path to success causes many students to become perfectionists and others to feel like they are never enough.

When marriages don't begin with setting proper expectations, couples constantly micromanage and nitpick one another. They aren't encouraging, and therefore, many don't last. Suppose I never communicate my expectations with my children and am continually critical of their actions. Our relationship will suffer. But when everyone knows the expectations, when we are given the autonomy to learn and make mistakes, and when we are encouraged to develop and improve, relationships grow stronger and will most certainly last.

Living a life of no regrets is never complete; it is never over, as we can always learn something new, gain a new perspective, and merely get better. A constant drive for mastery keeps life exciting and gives us something to look forward to. Once we believe we have learned it all and that we have fully arrived, things begin to fall apart. That's when we stop providing significance and where our influence will fade.

Building something that lasts isn't about motivation, and it isn't a one-time thing. It is a way of life that puts people above oneself so that others can become the best that they can be. Building something that lasts becomes the legacy that will live well beyond your years. You do this not to be seen, not to gain credit, but because it is the right thing to do.

## WHO DO YOU NEED TO ENCOURAGE?

## WHERE DO YOU NEED TO HOLD YOURSELF AND THOSE AROUND YOU ACCOUNTABLE?

## WHAT RELATIONSHIPS NEED TO GROW?

## WHAT IS YOUR PLAN TO ACCOMPLISH THESE THINGS? BE SPECIFIC.

Please visit our Distracted by Success Facebook page and let us know what you are building and how you are investing in people. Please share traditions that you've seen or do that make a difference in other people. Please help us all master the art of building something that lasts.

www.facebook.com/groups/distractedbysuccess/

# CONCLUSION:
## THE ILLUSION OF CHOICE
# CHAPTER 16: IF YOU WANT TO BE GREAT, THERE IS NO CHOICE

*"There is no Choice; Choice is an Illusion:"*
**Nick Saban**

As I wrap this book up, I want to highlight that I, like all people, have made several mistakes throughout my life and have many regrets. I also know I will make more mistakes as long as I live because that's just part of being human. But the thing is, the regrets that sting the most and that haunt me to this day all stemmed from me violating my deeply held values or playing the victim and living in the past or worrying about the future. My biggest regrets stem from my lack of action, fearing failure, or not doing what I knew I should have done. Many regrets were born out of selfish desires when I did things for my personal glory at the expense of others. My reason for writing this book is to help you not make these same types of mistakes. I hope that by reading this book, you have gained insight and built a plan that starts you on the road to a life without regret. One that will prevent you from making the same destructive decisions that plague many of us.

I know that when I age and get to the end of my life, there will be trips I wish I had gone on, there will be moments I wish I could do over, and there will be people I wish I could have met. I will be able to live with these disappointments so long as I live on the **Road to Success** as described in this book. I want to die knowing that I did all I could to live my values in every aspect of my life, having shared as much wisdom with all who wanted to hear. I want to arrive at death spent, filled with a ton of memories and great relationships, because I chased the right things instead of getting to the end of life with a large bank account and a lot of toys, yet completely drained and all alone, because I was running down the wrong road.

Below is a mantra that I feel encapsulates what it looks and feels like to live a life of no regrets.

"The Lions Chaser's Manifesto" by Mark Batterson. (Batterson, 22)

To live a life of no regrets, we must:

Quit living as if the purpose of life is to arrive safely at death.

Run to the Roar.

Set God-sized goals.

Pursue God-ordained passion.

Go after a dream that's destined to fail unless God intervenes.

Stop pointing out problems; become part of the solution.

Stop repeating the past and start creating the future.

Face your fears.

Fight for your dreams.

Grab opportunity by the mane, and don't let go.

Live like today is the first day and last day of your life.

Burn sinful bridges.

Blaze new trails.

Live for the applause of nail-scarred hands.

Don't let what's wrong with you keep you from worshipping what's right with God.

Don't try to be who you aren't.

Be yourself.
Laugh at yourself.
Dare to fail.
Dare to Dream.
Dare to be different.
Chase the lion!

To live like this, we must understand that there is no choice, for as former University of Alabama Head Football Coach Nick Saban said, "Choice is an illusion." You don't have a choice to be great, to be successful, or to become your best. You either know who you are, or you don't. You either live your values, or you don't. You are either optimistic, or you're not. You're either a person who does what they say, or you don't. You're either a person who builds things that last, or you aren't. There is no middle ground. You either do things that will make you great, make you a success, and remove regret, or you don't. There is no choice.

> YOU EITHER DO THINGS THAT WILL MAKE YOU GREAT, MAKE YOU A SUCCESS, AND REMOVE REGRET, OR YOU DON'T.

The path will not be easy, as many distractions will pop up along the way. It's at these times when we must be steadfast, stick to our values, and build something that lasts. I'm telling you, living a life to gain the applause of "Nail-scarred hands" will absolutely be worth it. What a joy it will be when we get to the end of our lives and realize we didn't miss it! Instead, we lived it without regret! And ultimately, hear the greatest words of all: well done, my good and faithful servant.

Thank you for reading this book and allowing me to encourage you. This message is so important because I have witnessed and continue to witness so many people live a distracted life. They are amazing people, but they get onto the wrong road, and it only leads to guilt. Thank you for letting me be a part of your life and speak into it. By reading this book, spending time in reflection, creating plans to get better, and executing them. You are now able to define true success so that it empowers you to live with no regrets in every aspect of your life.

## CALL TO ACTION:

I encourage you to go back through this book and read everything you wrote down. Pick out what matters most to you: your core values, your Standard, and your definition of success. Write these down on a notecard and place it on your nightstand or tape it to your bathroom mirror. Read it out loud every morning as a reminder of who you are, how you think, the actions you take, and what you are building. Look it over again every night and reflect: did you interact in all situations as your true self, sticking to your values no matter what life threw your way? Did you learn a new perspective, keep moving when times got difficult, and remain calm if things got challenging? Did you invest, coach, and encourage others to get better? Did you tackle your 1-2 top priorities of the day and let everything else fall into place? If you did, you could go to bed every night knowing that you had done all that you could to become a better person. Regardless of the outcomes of the day, regardless of the size of your bank account, your title, or your family's accomplishments, you will be a person without regret! You will have true success!

I pray that you stay focused on what really matters, live a life without regret, be full of joy and happiness, and leave a lasting legacy.

If you need a little nudge to get back on track, don't hesitate to reach out. We all need a little reminder now and then.

If you haven't done so, please join our "Distracted by Success" Facebook group. We would love to stay connected with you and hear your feedback on this book and how it has impacted your life. We are committed to becoming our best and to helping you do the same. Please get in touch with me and let us know how we can best help you!

www.facebook.com/groups/distractedbysuccess/

You have the tools and know what you need to do. Now, just go and do it!

Be a Champion Today.

# ACKNOWLEDGMENTS:

I want to thank all those who helped make this dream a reality. First, I want to express my profound gratitude to God for bringing me into this world and giving me the gift of teaching. I know that I cannot do anything without His divine guidance. I can't think of a better tribute than to write a book that I hope inspires many to follow a road of no regrets by pursuing the applause of nail-scared hands. This book is a testament to His grace, and I am deeply thankful for His role in its creation.

To my wife, Kerry, thank you for your endless hours of edits, revisions, vision, passion, and commitment to making this book as great as we could make it. At the same time, thank you for your support and belief in me. Life is so much more enjoyable when you know someone is in your corner rooting for you!

I want to thank my children, Parker, Karsyn, and McCade. They inspire me and hold me accountable for being who I say I will be. Above all, you three are what your mother and I are working to build that will last.

I want to thank my father, mother, stepdad, and siblings for their support and mentorship. I want to thank all those soul leaders who have impacted my life and helped to guide me into the man I am today. There are so many, but a special thanks to my grandfather, Leo McDonald, Jeff Callahan, Karl Kiefer, Jay Bell, Mike Wade, Thornton Kipper, Ian Moses, Bruce Kipper, Paul Mather, Brad Rogers, Joe Hadachek, Clint Hurdle, John Madia, Brad Larrondo, Bryan Harsin, the Social Studies Department from Mountain Pointe High School, Meg Austin, my mother-in-law, "Karen Jacobson," Jake Burton, Allen Peters, Jon Christiansen, Ryan Tranter, Scott Songer, Pat Dawson, all the coaches I have worked with and been coached by, all the young men that I coached while at Mountain Pointe, the 12U East Boise Blue Sox, all my friends, and many, many more.

I extend my heartfelt thanks to Dennis Welch and Gary Denham for their guidance and wisdom in editing this book, shaping the stories I used, and ensuring the seamless flow of the chapters.

I want to thank everyone who read my book before publishing it to ensure I got it right, especially Bryan Harsin, Gary Denham, Mike Wade, Joe Hadachek, Brad Rogers, Cole Tucker, and Vince Hordemann.

I want to thank my great friend, mentor, and soul leader, Clint Hurdle, for taking the time to write the foreword for this book. He is a person worth imitating.

A special thanks go to my "Who Friend," Bob Beaudine, for introducing me to some fantastic editors, reading my book, and providing a quote.

Thank you to Darleen Santore, "Coach Dar," Cole Tucker, and Bryan Harsin for attaching their names to my book with a quote.

Thank you, Floyd Orfield and A Books Mind, for helping me self-publish my first book and guiding me through this process.

Thank you, Eric Vanus and Eric Vanus Films, for creating a fantastic book trailer and helping me share this book and our brand with the world.

Thank you, Travis Jensen, for your friendship and encouragement and for organizing my book release party!

Thank you, Jeremy Buck and Lumuli Wanyonyi for encouraging me to write this book.

Finally, I want to express my deep appreciation to all my clients and all of you for taking a chance on me and this book. In a world full of options, I am humbled that you chose to invest a portion of your life in consuming the information I believe is pertinent to Your development and living a life with no regrets. Your engagement with this book is a testament to its impact, and I am truly grateful for your time and trust.

# AUTHOR BIO

Coach Buck

Brandon Buck is more than a coach. He embodies the definition of a coach as a sturdy carriage designed to transport people from one destination to another safely. This is Coach Buck. He is a person of faith, integrity, courage, persistence, responsibility, and action. These values are not just words for him but a way of life. He lives and breathes them, providing a stable and confident journey for people, teams, and organizations towards their desired destination. Coach Buck's unwavering commitment to his values is a testament to his dedication and reliability as a coach.

As a Husband, Father, Author, Speaker, Teacher, Coach, and CEO/Owner of Infinite Strengths, Brandon has helped his family, athletes, CEOs, Fortune 100 and 500 companies, and leaders simplify their actions to succeed personally and professionally. He helps create clarity around their identity and actions so they are productive instead of merely busy. He helps teams cut out the noise, provides an environment where people can be honest with themselves, and then holds them accountable to their plan. He ensures he and his clients prioritize and nurture their most precious relationships, emphasizing their importance and the impact they can have on personal and professional success. His authenticity and simple yet direct questioning have helped many people begin and continue living a life of no regrets.

# BIBLIOGRAPHY:

Arnett, Dale, and Rick Dikeman. "John Wooden." *Wikipedia*, Wikimedia Foundation, 17 Feb. 2024, en.wikipedia.org/wiki/John_Wooden.

Haden, Jeff. "Richard Branson Says 1 Thing Separates Successful People from All the Rest (and Leads to Living a Happy and Fulfilling Life) | Inc.Com." *Inc. Com*, 2023, www.inc.com/jeff-haden/richard-branson-says-1-thing-separates-successful-people-from-all-rest-and-leads-to-living-a-happy-fulfilling-life. html.

Scipioni, Jade. "At 8, Derek Jeter Knew He Wanted to Play for the Yankees-Here's How He Made It Happen." *CNBC*, CNBC, 22 Jan. 2020, www.cnbc. com/2020/01/21/former-new-york-yankees-derek-jeters-10-lessons-for-suc-cess.html.

Earthman, Average, and Brian Brockmeyer. "Derek Jeter: Revision History." *Wikipe-dia*, Wikimedia Foundation, 2004, en.wikipedia.org/w/index.php?title=Der-ek_Jeter&action=history&dir=prev&offset=20040905061158%7C5819303.

Wylleman, Paul, and David Lavallee. "(PDF) A Developmental Perspective on Transitions Faced by Athletes." *A Developmental Perspective on Transitions Face by Athletes*, researchgate.net, 2021, www.researchgate.net/publica-tion/354209101_A_Developmental_Perspective_on_Transitions_Faced_by_

Athletes.

Marcus, Jonathan J. "What We Can Learn from a Styrofoam Cup." *HIGH-PER-FORMANCE WEST*, HIGH PERFORMANCE WEST, 20 Mar. 2018, www.highperformancewest.com/blog/2018/3/20/what-we-can-learn-from-a-styrofoam-cup.

Rosen, Jeffery. "Opioid Manufacturer Purdue Pharma Pleads Guilty to Fraud and Kickback Conspiracies." *Office of Public Affairs | Opioid Manufacturer Purdue Pharma Pleads Guilty to Fraud and Kickback Conspiracies | United States Department of Justice*, 24 Nov. 2020, www.justice.gov/opa/pr/opioid-manufacturer-purdue-pharma-pleads-guilty-fraud-and-kickback-conspiracies.

Vigdor, Neil. "The Houston Astros' 2017 Cheating Scandal: What Happened." *The New York Times*, The New York Times, 14 Jan. 2020, www.nytimes.com/article/astros-cheating.html.

Moawad, Trevor. *It Takes What It Takes: How to Manage Negativity, Thrive in Chaos, and Conquer Any Goal*. HarperCollins Publishers, 2020.

Panchanathan, Sethuraman. "National Science Foundation." *NSF*, 20 Mar. 2024, www.nsf.gov/.

Douglass, Frederick. "Frederick Douglass - Narrative, Quotes & Facts." *History. Com*, A&E Television Networks, 2009, www.history.com/topics/black-history/frederick-douglass.

Kupietzky, Joshua. "History: How a Cancelled Flight Prompted the Formation of Virgin Atlantic." *Simple Flying*, 17 Sept. 2023, simpleflying.com/virgin-atlantic-origin-story/#:~:text=Branson%20believed%20enough%20people%20wanted,he%20needed%20was%20the%20aircraft.&text=This%20prompted%20Branson%20to%20go,and%20filled%20up%20an%20aircraft.

"US Obesity Rates Have Tripled over the Last 60 Years." *USAFacts*, USAFacts, 21 Mar. 2023, usafacts.org/articles/obesity-rate-nearly-triples-united-states-over-last-50-years/.

Organization. "Nearly Half of American Households Have No Retirement Savings." *USAFacts*, USAFacts, 9 Nov. 2023, usafacts.org/data-projects/retirement-savings.

Harper, Brenna. "Divorce Statistics in 2024 (Latest U.S. Data)." *Maze of Love*, 15 Jan. 2024, mazeoflove.com/divorce/.

Impelman, Craig, and Name. "Never Mistake Activity for Achievement." *Coach John Wooden*, 18 Oct. 2023, www.thewoodeneffect.com/activity-achievement/#:~:text=The%20four%20components%20Coach%20Wooden,his%20book%20Practical%20Modern%20Basketball.

Robbins, Tony. "The #1 Rule for Lasting Results." *Tonyrobbins.Com*, 28 Nov. 2023, www.tonyrobbins.com/productivity-performance/number-one-rule-for-results/#:~:text=But%20whether%20it's%20getting%20healthy,the%20second%20week%20of%20January.

Almanac, Baseball. "Major League Baseball Player Encyclopedia." *Baseball Almanac*, 2024, www.baseball-almanac.com/players/ballplayer.shtml#:~:text=Did%20you%20know%20that%20through,debuted%20in%20the%20National%20League.

Pillemer, Karl. "How to Live Life without Regrets: 8 Lessons from Older Americans." *TODAY.Com*, TODAY, 31 Dec. 2019, www.today.com/health/biggest-regrets-older-people-share-what-they-d-do-differently-t118918.

Buettner, Dan. "Blue Zones, Lessons for Living Longer." *Blue Zones*, Blue Zones, 6 June 2010, www.bluezones.com/dan-buettner/.

"Loneliness and Social Isolation Linked to Serious Health Conditions." *Centers for Disease Control and Prevention*, Centers for Disease Control and Prevention, 29 Apr. 2021, www.cdc.gov/aging/publications/features/lonely-older-adults.html.

"San Mateo County Becomes 1st in Us to Declare Loneliness as Health Emergency."

*ABC7 San Francisco*, 31 Jan. 2024, abc7news.com/san-mateo-declares-lone-liness-state-of-emergency-first-in-us-mental-health-depression/14373042/.

Batterson, Mark. "Lion Chaser's Manifesto." *Mark Batterson*, 22 Feb. 2022, www.markbatterson.com/books/chase-the-lion/.

Duke, Jeff. *3D Coach*. Revell, a Division of Baker Publishing Group, 2014.

Biderman, David. "11 Minutes of Action." *Wall Street Journal*, 2010, www.wsj.com.

Wooden, John R., and Jay Carty. *Coach Wooden's Pyramid of Success: Building Blocks for a Better Life*. Revell, a Division of Baker Publishing Group, 2015.

Printed in the USA
CPSIA information can be obtained
at www.ICGtesting.com
CBHW070009270524
9043CB00009B/14